THE COMING
 OF THE FRENCH
REVOLUTION

THE COMING

OF THE

FRENCH

REVOLUTION

BY GEORGES LEFEBVRE

Translated and with a preface by

R. R. PALMER

With a new introduction by

TIMOTHY TACKETT

PRINCETON UNIVERSITY PRESS

PRINCETON AND OXFORD

Copyright © 1947, renewed 1975 by Princeton University Press
New introduction Copyright © 2005 by Princeton University Press
Published by Princeton University Press, 41 William Street,
Princeton, New Jersey 08540
In the United Kingdom: Princeton University Press,
3 Market Place, Woodstock, Oxfordshire OX20 1SY

First published in English in 1947
First paperback edition, 1967
First expanded Bicentennial edition, 1988
First Princeton Classic Edition, with a new introduction by Timothy
Tackett, 2005

This work was first published in French, under the title *Quatre-vingt-
neuf*, in 1939 under the auspices of the Institute for the History of the
French Revolution, University of Paris, in conjunction with the National
Committee for the Celebration of the 150th Anniversary of the French
Revolution.

Library of Congress Cataloging-in-Publication Data

Lefebvre, Georges, 1874–1959.
[Quatre-vingt-neuf. English]
The coming of the French Revolution / by Georges Lefebvre ; translated
and with a preface by R.R. Palmer.—1st Princeton classic ed. / with a new
introduction by Timothy Tackett.
p.   cm.
Includes bibliographical references and index.
ISBN-13: 978-0-691-12188-8 (pbk.)
ISBN-10: 0-691-12188-5 (pbk.)
1. France—History—Revolution, 1789–1799—Causes. I. Title.
DC138.L4513 2005
944.04'1—dc22   2005040861

British Library Cataloging-in-Publication Data is available

This book has been composed in Minion
Printed on acid-free paper. ∞
pup.princeton.edu

Printed in the United States of America

10   9   8   7   6   5   4

Contents

Introduction BY TIMOTHY TACKETT

THE Revolution that occurred in France in the last decade of the eighteenth century was one of the pivotal moments in the recent history of the Western world. The modern concepts of liberalism, nationalism, republicanism, feminism, abolitionism, and de-Christianization were all powerfully influenced and propagated, if not invented, by the French Revolution. This event took place, moreover, not in an obscure country on the fringes of Western culture, or in a nation in decline, but in one of the world's great powers, with economic strength, military might, and cultural influence second to none. Indeed, once the new regime turned outward and became expansionist, the Revolutionary state and the Napoleonic imperium that followed profoundly disrupted and sometimes transformed regimes throughout Europe and the Atlantic world.

Perhaps no single issue concerning this extraordinary event has seemed more puzzling than the problem of its origins in 1789. How was it that such a vast upheaval broke out in the first place? Was it a question of material suffering or a sense of injustice and envy between different social groups in France? Or did it come about through the power of a new ideology or through an internal breakdown of central

The author gratefully acknowledges the advice and assistance of James Friguglietti, T. G. A. Le Goff, and Helen Chenut.

authority or even through the conspiracy of a small minority of dedicated fanatics? Like the fall of Rome or the rise of capitalism, the origins of the French Revolution have been debated again and again, with interpretations invariably colored by the problems and perspectives prominent in each generation. Indeed, in France itself an understanding of the Revolution and its origins was linked to the very concept of national identity, and a whole series of statesmen-writers— from François Guizot, Louis Blanc, and Alphonse de Lamartine to Alexis de Tocqueville, Adolphe Thiers, and Jean Jaurès—felt compelled to confront and write at length on this moment in their nation's past.

Only toward the end of the nineteenth century did the history of the Revolution become an academic discipline. The first scholarly review consecrated to the subject was created in 1881, and ten years later a chair in the Revolution was established at the University of Paris. Thereafter a series of remarkable French specialists (from Alphonse Aulard and Albert Mathiez at the beginning of the twentieth century to Albert Soboul and Michel Vovelle at the end) wrote, directed, or inspired thousands of carefully documented archival studies on almost every aspect of the Revolutionary experience, not only in Paris but in hundreds of regions and towns throughout the country. Yet even with this great accumulation of writings and new knowledge, the resolution of the problem of the Revolution's outbreak remained elusive.

I

In this long and distinguished line of historians, no one grappled longer and harder with the origins of 1789, no one attained a greater mastery of both the archives and the scholarly literature of the Revolution, than the author of the present study, Georges Lefebvre.

Lefebvre's life spanned virtually the entire period of the French Third and Fourth Republics.[1] Born in 1874 in the industrial city of Lille near the Belgian border, he was the son of a minor accountant for a commercial firm, the grandson of a simple textile worker. With such modest family resources, he was able to attend school only by means of a series of scholarships, and he could never afford studies in Paris. Moreover, the peculiarities of his education in Lille led him to concentrate on modern languages, science, and mathematics rather than on the Latin, Greek, and philosophy that formed the core curriculum in France's elite institutions. Though such an education made it more difficult for Lefebvre to penetrate the Parisian intellectual elite, it would also make him more open than most of his contemporaries to scholarship published outside France and to the application of the social sciences and statistics to history.

At the University of Lille his earliest love was for medieval English history. The eminent medievalist Charles Petit-Dutaillis took on the young Lefebvre as a "collaborator" in the publication of a French edition of William Stubbs's massive constitutional history of medieval England. Lefebvre did the

[1] A biography of Lefebvre remains to be written. Among the principal sources for the following paragraphs are Georges Lefebvre, "Pro Domo," *Annales historiques de la Révolution française* [hereafter cited as *AHRF*] (1947): 188–90; and "Allocution [on his eightieth birthday]," *La Pensée. Revue du rationalisme moderne*, no. 69 (May–June 1955): 27–34. See also the series of articles commemorating Lefebvre's death in *AHRF* 32 (1960): 1–128; Richard Cobb, "Georges Lefebvre," in *A Second Identity: Essays on France and French History* (London, 1969), 84–100; P. L'Huillier, "Georges Lefebvre à Strasbourg," *Bulletin de la Faculté des lettres de l'Université de Strasbourg* 38 (1959–60): 371–76; Jacques Godechot, *Un jury pour la Révolution* (Paris, 1974), 311–22; and Michel Vovelle, *Combats pour la Révolution française* (Paris, 1993), 33–43. Lawrence Harvard Davis, "Georges Lefebvre: Historian and Public Intellectual, 1928–1959" (Ph.D. diss., University of Connecticut, 2001), is particularly useful for its bibliography. A full *Bibliographie de Georges Lefebvre* was published by James Friguglietti (Paris, 1972).

entire translation from the English—well over two thousand pages of text and notes—and added a lengthy supplement to the final volume, summarizing with immense erudition works published on the subject since Stubbs's death, a supplement that would later be translated into English.[2]

It seems to have been sometime after he had passed the *agrégation* examination in 1899 and had completed his requisite military service that he discovered the French Revolution. Of particular importance in this conversion, as he would recall many years later, was his encounter with the multivolume "socialist" history of the Revolution written by the political leader and statesman Jean Jaurès. Though he never met Jaurès personally, and saw him only twice, listening to his speeches in the midst of great crowds, he would always refer to Jaurès as his "teacher."[3]

Since his youth Lefebvre had been nurtured on the Marxist theories of Jules Guesde, the representative from Lille to the French National Assembly. But he seems to have found a particular affinity with Jaurès's less doctrinaire brand of Marxism. He joined the unified socialist party (the S.F.I.O.), founded by Jaurès in 1905, and maintained his membership to the end of the Third Republic, even after the formation of the more radical Communist Party in 1920. Through his early readings and his political initiation, Lefebvre came firmly to believe in the importance of Karl Marx's understanding of social class in the development of history. Yet throughout his life such convictions existed in a curious and complex tension with his commitment to the positivist,

---

[2] William Stubbs, *L'histoire constitutionnelle de l'Angleterre, son origine et son développement*, 3 vols. (Paris, 1907, 1913, and 1927); also Charles Petit-Dutaillis and Georges Lefebvre, *Studies and Notes Supplementary to Stubbs' Constitutional History* (Manchester, 1930).

[3] Jean Jaurès, *Histoire socialiste, 1789–1900*, 13 vols. (Paris, 1901–8). The first four volumes written by Jaurès (1901–4) dealt with the Revolution. Also, Lefebvre, "Pro Domo," 188.

empirical approach to history that he had learned from Petit-Dutaillis. He was a voracious but meticulous researcher, who always promoted careful erudition and pursued it himself with almost obsessive dedication: "without erudition there can be no history." He looked for inspiration in Descartes' *Discourse on Method* as much as in the social theories of Marx, and he would be critical of Soviet historians for "confusing history and propaganda." As one of his students described him in the late 1940s, "he was not really at ease with doctrine."[4]

Inspired by Jaurès's history "from below," Lefebvre threw himself into a massive doctoral thesis on the peasantry in the region near Lille (the *département* of Nord) before and during the Revolution. The completion of the work was long delayed by World War I, since he was forced to abandon his research notes during the German invasion and occupation of Lille and then served for a time in the army home guard (though he was now over forty). But when he recovered his notes at the end of the war and was finally able to complete and publish the study in 1924, the work became one of the most remarkable and influential doctoral theses in French history.[5] Lefebvre not only created the modern field of peasant studies but also pioneered many of the approaches later promoted by the celebrated *Annales* school of history. It was a massive local study of the rural population developed through a layered analysis: first of the geography, then of the socioeconomic "structures" and landholding patterns, then of the "culture" of agricultural practices and peasant life, and finally of the "event" of the French Revolution and its transformation of both the structures and the culture of the peasant's world. Throughout, the analysis was

---

[4] Cobb, "Georges Lefebvre," 56 and 62; Madeleine Rebérioux in *AHRF* 32 (1960): 79.

[5] *Les paysans du Nord pendant la Révolution française* (Paris, 1924).

buttressed by extensive statistical tables—all produced by laborious hand calculation.

It was only after the defense of this thesis at the Sorbonne, at age fifty, that Lefebvre was able to leave secondary-school teaching and become a university professor, first in the small town of Clermont-Ferrand and then in the more important post of Strasbourg. His eight years in Strasbourg were among the most creative and prolific of his career. In rapid succession, he completed a first synthesis on the French Revolution—published in 1930 in collaboration with Philippe Sagnac and Raymond Guyot—a study of agrarian problems during the Terror, and a massive overview on the Napoleonic age.[6] But perhaps the single most important work of this period was his study of the Great Fear, the momentous chain-reaction panic that swept across much of France in July and August 1789.[7] With extraordinarily patient erudition pursued both in Paris and in local archives, he was able to reconstruct the origins and currents of the various panics and propose a complex explanation based on social and political conditions, the nature of communications networks, and the psychology of fear and rumor. Lefebvre's innovative approach to history and his interest in popular mentality probably both influenced and were influenced by two remarkable colleagues at Strasbourg, Marc Bloch and Lucien Febvre, who founded their pathbreaking historical review, the *Annales d'histoire économique et sociale*, soon after his arrival there.[8]

---

[6] Georges Lefebvre, Raymond Guyot, and Philippe Sagnac, *La Révolution française*, vol. 13 of *Peuples et Civilisations* (Paris, 1930); *Questions agraires au temps de la Terreur* (Strasbourg, 1932); *Napoléon*, trans. Henry F. Stockhold and J. E. Anderson, 2 vols. (New York, 1969; originally published in French in 1935).

[7] *The Great Fear of 1789: Rural Panic in Revolutionary France*, trans. Joan White (New York, 1973; originally published in French in 1932).

[8] First published in 1929. Still appearing today under the title *Annales. Histoire et sciences sociales*.

In 1935, at the age of sixty-one, Lefebvre was finally named to a professorship in Paris. Two years later he took over the chair in the French Revolution at the Sorbonne (in 1932 at the death of Albert Mathiez he had already assumed editorship of the most important French Revolutionary review, the *Annales historiques de la Révolution française*). It was a moment of great turmoil and political confrontation in the university and in France generally. Passionately committed to defending republican and democratic values in the face of fascism, he founded and served as president of the Cercle Descartes, a group of university and secondary-school teachers dedicated to promoting free and rational discussion on the issues of the time. With the support of the left-leaning Popular Front government, he also threw himself into preparations for the 150th anniversary of the Revolution. He took part in a series of radio broadcasts on the subject and served as historical adviser for Jean Renoir's celebrated film on the Revolution, *La Marseillaise*. It was in 1939, on the very eve of World War II, that he published the present study of the origins of the French Revolution, conceived as his contribution to the anniversary commemoration.[9]

The war years were a sad and difficult time for Lefebvre. The tragedy of France's defeat in 1940 was compounded by the sudden death of his wife in 1941 and the execution by the Nazis of his brother Théodore, a university professor in Poitiers, and his close Jewish friends, Marc Bloch and Maurice Halbwachs—the first shot near Lyon, the second killed in a German concentration camp. But he carried on with his teaching at the Sorbonne, continuing well after his normal retirement age, for fear that the German occupiers might take the occasion to abolish the chair on the French Revolution. He also pushed on with the preparation of a major publication of

[9] *Quatre-Vingt-Neuf* (Paris, 1939). His other major publication of this period was *Les Thermidoriens* (Paris, 1937).

documents on the origins of the Revolution, giving employment to a number of graduate students, attempting to protect
them in this way from forced factory work in Germany.[10]

Although he retired from the Sorbonne soon after the
war, he stayed on as editor of the *Annales historiques de la
Révolution française* and as director of the university institute for the study of the Revolution, which he had founded
in 1937. In 1946 he published a study of the Directory period
(1795–99), and in 1951 he brought out an extensively rewrit-
ten version of his general synthesis on the age of the French
Revolution.[11] Though there is some suggestion that he moved
closer to communism during this period, he never joined
the Communist Party and maintained his nondoctrinaire
position on Marxism to the end of his life. He spent most of
his final years in his small house in the working-class town
of Boulogne-sur-Seine, southwest of Paris, a house that
became a destination for aspiring French Revolutionary
scholars from around the world.

The British historian Richard Cobb, who frequently visited
him in Boulogne, has left us an unforgettable description of
Lefebvre in his eighties. With his small white goatee, piercing
blue eyes, and the light complexion of northern France
(which turned purple, however, at the mention of Marie-
Antoinette), he sat at a desk piled high with books, positioned
between a portrait of Jaurès and a bust of Robespierre. He

---

[10] Eventually published as Georges Lefebvre and Anne Terroine, eds.,
Recueil de documents relatifs aux séances des Etats généraux, 2 vols. (Paris,
1953–62). For information on Lefebvre's activities during World War II,
I have also relied on a personal conversation with Olga Ilovaïsky, one of
his assistants during this period.

[11] The first was grouped with his 1937 publication and translated as *The
Thermidorians and the Directory: Two Phases of the French Revolution*,
trans. Robert Baldick (New York, 1964); the second as *The French Revolution*, trans. Elizabeth Moss Evanson, John Hall Stewart, and James
Friguglietti, 2 vols. (New York, 1962–64).

was the "living embodiment of republican rectitude, of lay probity, a sort of French Abraham Lincoln, dressed in antiquated clothes."[12] He died in 1959 in his eighty-sixth year, pursuing his writing and research to the end.

II

         The Coming of the French Revolution, originally entitled *Quatre-Vingt-Neuf* (Eighty-nine), was written by Lefebvre in 1939 at the pinnacle of his career. It was self-consciously conceived for a broader audience of students and the general public and was published without the scholarly apparatus of footnotes and bibliography. Yet it represented the sum of a lifetime of reflection on the origins and meaning of the events of 1789.

         As the reader will discover, much of the book's persuasive power comes from its brilliant and elegant construction. The first two-thirds of the study are organized around a sequence of "four acts," as Lefebvre himself describes them, each associated with one of four major groupings in French society. The first act, the "Aristocratic Revolution," began in 1787 when elements of the French nobility, working first through the provincial parlements and estates and then through an Assembly of Notables, forced King Louis XVI to convoke a national representative body, the Estates General. In Lefebvre's view, this action capped several decades of "aristocratic reaction" in which the nobility attempted both to regain political power lost to the royalty in the seventeenth century and to reassert its social position in the face of a rising middle class or "bourgeoisie"—by reinvigorating its seigneurial rights and closing off entry by commoners to all positions of authority in the kingdom. But in successfully

---

[12] Cobb, "Georges Lefebvre," 52.

weakening the royal government, the aristocracy opened the door to the second act of the drama, a very different revolution of the bourgeoisie. The latter group began mobilizing politically in the fall of 1788 and effectively took over the Estates General in May and June 1789, transforming that body into a sovereign National Assembly. Thereafter, in the third and fourth "acts," first the popular classes of Paris and then the rural peasantry successively mounted the stage of history, each promoting its own somewhat separate revolutionary goals. But while the bourgeois leaders, the people of Paris, and the peasants often pursued different objectives, they were bound together in their common hatred and suspicion of the very aristocrats who had launched the Revolution. Indeed, all three groups of commoners, Lefebvre believed, were obsessed with the idea of an "aristocratic conspiracy" in which the nobles were thought to be planning an attack against the nation. This conspiracy obsession, in Lefebvre's view, "is one of the keys of the history of the Revolution," influencing both the attack on the Bastille on July 14 and the peasant insurrections against the seigneurial system that exploded during the summer.

Yet the climax of the book comes not with the descriptions of the social dramas of 1789, but rather in part 5 with Lefebvre's analysis of two foundation acts crafted by the National Assembly: the declaration of August 4 abolishing "feudalism" and the Declaration of the Rights of Man and the Citizen of August 26. Even though in Lefebvre's view these twin decrees emerged from the ideology of the bourgeois class—as expressed in the eighteenth century by the philosophers of the Enlightenment—they were conceived as having universal meaning applicable to all classes in society.[13] It is in this sense that the two declarations constituted "the essential work of the Revolution of 1789."

[13] Note that Lefebvre never actually uses the word "Enlightenment" in his text.

Part 6 of the book appears almost as an epilogue and presents Lefebvre's version of the so-called October Days (October 5–6, 1789). This tumultuous series of events originated, in his view, when the bourgeois leaders of the assembly decided on the need to administer a "second dose of revolution" to Louis XVI, encouraging the Parisian masses, women and men, to march on the royal palace in Versailles. In this way the king was compelled to accept the August declarations and to take up residence in Paris, thus bringing the Revolution of 1789 to a close.

Yet beneath the book's simple, almost classical architecture lies a deceptively complex analysis of the causes and early development of the Revolution. Perhaps more than in any of Lefebvre's other major works, there is a tension between the conceptual assumption of the primacy of economic class and the positivist imperative of basing all assertions on empirical research. In his notion of the "four revolutions" of 1789, each associated with a specific social group or class, Lefebvre made a substantial departure both from the syntheses of Jaurès and Mathiez and from his own earlier overview of 1930. Significantly, the "bourgeois revolution" of *The Coming of the French Revolution* was described in 1930 as the "jurists' revolution"; the "peasant revolution" was previously termed an "agrarian revolt." At times in the text printed here Lefebvre seems almost to personify each of the four social actors, as though they were single individuals: "the bourgeoisie" or "the aristocracy" or "the people" are said to have such-and-such thoughts or to make such-and-such decisions. Nevertheless, Lefebvre also went to great lengths to demonstrate the multiple components and even contradictory attitudes coexisting within each of those social groups—only two of which, the bourgeoisie and the aristocracy, were actually referred to as "classes." It is clear from his analysis, moreover, that there was a great deal of interaction among the four groups throughout 1788 and 1789. In this sense, Lefebvre's successive "acts" describe periods in which one group was the most important but not the sole actor in the revolutionary drama.

In addition, Lefebvre's understanding of the origins of the Revolution was very much dependent on the level of analysis and the chronological perspective under consideration. He anticipated Fernand Braudel's distinction between short-term and long-term developments (*temps court* vs. *longue durée*). The opening paragraphs of the book emphasize the "ultimate" or "deeper" causes of the Revolution in phrases that might have come from the *Communist Manifesto* of Karl Marx and Friedrich Engels. For centuries, it is argued, a growing contradiction had developed between the political and social domination of an aristocratic class, whose power was based in its ownership of land, and the emerging class of the bourgeoisie, characterized by its control of a new kind of mobile wealth originating in commerce and industry. This social contradiction was pushing inexorably toward a class confrontation that would restore "the harmony between fact and law."

Yet after the initial invocation of a Marxist *longue durée*, Lefebvre rapidly modulates to the problem of the "immediate," shorter-term causes of the Revolution that is the primary subject of the book and of fundamental importance in his explanation of why the Revolution occurred at this moment and why it assumed the specific character that it did. In the course of the book's development and conclusion, at least five other factors are designated as direct "causes" affecting the origins of the Revolution in a major way: the collapse of the central government; the personalities of the king and queen; the American Revolution; the climatic disasters of 1788 and the consequent economic distress; and the writings of the French philosophers of the eighteenth century. Lefebvre also gives significant weight to the economic, administrative, and cultural centralization of France and even to the long-term impact of a Christian concept of individualism. All such elements were further complicated, moreover, by the decisions of the king and of a succession of individual ministers who, in their conflicts with the aristocracy, were not averse to using a "revolutionary language" of their own. In fact, the royal government frequently appears in the book as a veritable fifth independent actor, sharing the stage with the aristocracy, the bourgeoisie, the people of Paris, and the peasantry.

Summarizing in his conclusion the Revolutionary actions of the French in 1789, Lefebvre underlines the intricate mix of motives: "Class interests and personal interests, humbled pride, mass suffering, philosophical propaganda all made their contributions, in proportions different for each individual, but with the net effect of producing . . . a collective mentality that was strangely complex." Indeed, some of the most striking and insightful pages in the book emphasize the peculiar psychological traits of the bourgeoisie, the masses of Paris, and the peasant populations, and explore how these led the Revolution to take the particular course that it did. Rumor, fear (of both real and imagined threats), utopian expectations, envy, fear of envy, desire for revenge: all played a role in the course of events in 1789. Set beside the complex and sophisticated analysis that characterizes most of the book, the occasional slippage into a simplistic language of reified class seems somewhat discordant and inconsistent.

In any case, Lefebvre's agenda in writing the book was complicated by two other implicit goals. First, certain aspects of his analysis were undoubtedly colored by events in France in the late 1930s. This presentist perspective is particularly evident in the conclusion, where he takes care to delineate the differences between fascism, on the one hand, and the values of the French Revolution, on the other. As he described it in early 1940 to his Swiss friend Alfred Rufer, the book was dedicated to advancing "the cause of liberty." This was the origin of the concluding appeal to the French youth of his day, urging them to seek inspiration not in fascism but in the glorious heritage of the Revolution. But one can also perceive the impact of the French Popular Front of 1936 in Lefebvre's eagerness to emphasize elements of unity among the three major classes of commoners, notably in their putative opposition to an "aristocratic conspiracy" and in their subscription to the universal message of the Declaration of Rights. Given the implicit and explicit antifascist message of the text, it is hardly surprising that the book was condemned and systematically burned by the Germans after they occupied France in 1940.[14]

A second implicit goal of the book is to reflect on the links between the events of 1789 and the period of the Terror of 1793–94. Lefebvre rejects the distinction made by some historians between a "good" Revolution of 1789–90 and a Revolution that somehow went astray after 1791 or 1792. One could speculate—and Lefebvre does so briefly—on how 1789 might have led to a peaceful evolutionary transformation in the direction of democracy, similar to that which occurred in England. But for the most part he eschews such speculations. He carefully explores the violent propensities of the Revolutionary crowds, their fear of conspiracy, their "will to punish" the perceived enemies of the nation. In the end, however, it was the complete lack of statesmanship on the part of Louis XVI and the unalterable opposition of the great bulk of the aristocracy that made violence unavoidable. Lefebvre ultimately adheres to the assessment of the Third Republic

---

[14] "Correspondance d'Albert Mathiez et de Georges Lefebvre avec Alfred Rufer," *AHRF* 51 (1979): 436. See also the lecture given by Lefebvre at the time he was writing the book: "Les principes de 1789 dans le monde actuel," *Cahiers du Cercle Descartes*, no. 9 (1939): 5–20. Lefebvre gave all the proceeds he received from the book to charity: Cobb, "Georges Lefebvre," 54. On the destruction of the French edition, see Robert Palmer's preface to the first edition of *The Coming of the French Revolution* (Princeton, 1947).

leader Georges Clemenceau, that "the Revolution is a *bloc*, a single thing."

III

For a half century after its publication, *The Coming of the French Revolution* was probably the single most influential book in the world on the origins of the French Revolution. In conjunction with Lefebvre's general synthesis of 1951—which summarized most of its conclusions—the book established an interpretive paradigm with enormous impact both in fixing an agenda for future research and in setting the terms of scholarly debate.

At the time of his death, Lefebvre received a remarkable series of tributes from around the world. Historians from England, Germany, Italy, Japan, and Russia all professed their admiration for his work and testified to its influence on Revolutionary studies pursued in their countries. Similar words of praise came from many of the major American specialists of eighteenth-century France, including Robert Palmer, Beatrice Hyslop, Leo Gershoy, Crane Brinton, and Harold Parker—all of whom had met Lefebvre in France and consulted him on their research.[15] As early as 1939, Palmer had arranged to produce an English version of *Quatre-Vingt-Neuf*, though because of the war, he was unable to bring out the publication until 1947. Thereafter, and in no small measure owing to Palmer's remarkable translation, the book would become basic reading for several generations of American and other English-speaking readers, remaining in print continuously from 1947 to the present.

Within the academic milieu in France, Lefebvre's work and his explanation of the origins of the Revolution long stood as

[15] *AHRF* 32 (1960): 1–128.

the unquestioned canon in the field. The *Annales historiques de la Révolution française* published renewed tributes to the master on both the tenth and the twentieth anniversaries of his death, and an international colloquium was organized in Paris on the fifteenth anniversary, dedicated to the memory of both Lefebvre and Mathiez.[16] Albert Soboul, who had been Lefebvre's student and who assumed the chair in the French Revolution in 1967, passionately defended his teacher's interpretations, though he also tended to give them a much more rigid Marxist reading. He published a new French edition of *The Coming of the French Revolution* in 1970 with an elaborate introduction and afterword.[17]

Yet beginning even before his death and continuing through the end of the twentieth century, an array of historians would call into question various aspects of the explanatory paradigm identified most closely with Lefebvre. The most prominent attacks came from a loose coalition of critics, soon widely referred to as "revisionists" and initially dominated by a younger generation of British and American historians. Much of their work was based on new empirical research that claimed to invalidate the Marxist aspects of Lefebvre's analysis, especially the concepts of an "aristocratic reaction" at the end of the Old Regime and a "bourgeois revolution" in 1789.[18] As

[16] *AHRF* 41 (1969): 549–69; and 51 (1979): 357–442; Albert Soboul, ed., *Voies nouvelles pour l'histoire de la Révolution française. Colloque Albert Mathiez–Georges Lefebvre* (Paris, 1978).

[17] Georges Lefebvre, *Quatre-Vingt-Neuf* (Paris, 1970).

[18] It would be impossible here to develop all of the arcane debates between the "orthodox" historians and their "revisionist" critics. For a more thorough development, see, e.g., William Doyle, *Origins of the French Revolution* (Oxford, 1980), 7–40; Michel Vovelle, "L'historiographie de la Révolution française à la veille du bicentenaire," *AHRF* 60 (1988): 113–26; and Norman Hampson, "The French Revolution and Its Historians," in *The Permanent Revolution: The French Revolution and Its Legacy, 1789–1989*, ed. Geoffrey Best (London, 1988), 211–34.

early as the 1950s the British historian Alfred Cobban questioned how the Revolution of 1789 could be termed "bourgeois," when the Third Estate deputies who created the
National Assembly were primarily lawyers, judges, and other
professional men. Through a careful statistical analysis he
demonstrated that members of the eighteenth-century bourgeoisie by Lefebvre's own definition—merchants, manufacturers, bankers, and the like—constituted scarcely more than
10 percent of the Third Estate representatives. Elizabeth
Eisenstein continued in a similar vein in 1965, with a critique
of Lefebvre's analysis of the individuals who led the "bourgeois" mobilization in the fall of 1788, suggesting on the basis
of Lefebvre's own text that they were primarily great aristocrats and clergymen. About the same time George Taylor
questioned the very basis of the class analysis at the heart of
Lefebvre's understanding of the "ultimate" causes of the Revolution. After extensive new research on the structures of wealth
in Old Regime France, he concluded that nobles and commoners had almost identical forms of income. While both
groups had placed some of their investments in merchant
capitalism, the bulk of their revenues were drawn from identical forms of proprietary wealth.[19]

Other historians set their sights on Lefebvre's contention
that the French nobility was closing itself off in the course of
the eighteenth century. They demonstrated empirically that the
composition of the power elites—in the administration, in
the army, in the church, in the magistracy—had changed very
little since the reign of Louis XIV in the seventeenth century,

[19] Alfred Cobban, *The Myth of the French Revolution* (London, 1955);
and *The Social Interpretation of the French Revolution* (Cambridge, 1964);
Elizabeth L. Eisenstein, "Who Intervened? A Commentary on *The Coming of
the French Revolution*," *American Historical Review* 71 (1965): 77–103; George
V. Taylor, "Types of Capitalism in Eighteenth-Century France," *English Historical Review* 79 (1964): 478–97; and "Noncapitalist Wealth and the Origins
of the French Revolution," *American Historical Review* 72 (1967): 469–96.

and that substantial numbers of commoners continued to
enter the nobility during the last century of the Old Regime.
Additional criticisms came from those who questioned
Lefebvre's tight identification of the ideas of the Enlightenment with the bourgeois class, an assertion that seemed
dubious given the substantial representation of the nobility
among writers of the period and in salons, academies,
Masonic lodges, and other forms of Enlightened sociability.
In 1980, on the basis of such studies and of his own research,
William Doyle launched a frontal attack against the Lefebvre
paradigm, disputing the whole concept of an "aristocratic
reaction," and arguing that in 1789 there had been neither a
social crisis nor an economic crisis—beyond the "accident
of nature" caused by hailstorms in the summer of 1788.[20]

However, the revisionists were probably more successful
in criticizing certain aspects of Lefebvre's interpretation
than in developing alternative proposals of their own. In
general, both Doyle and Taylor stressed the political origins
of 1789, the extent to which an internal breakdown of the
Old Regime government opened the door to what "was
essentially a political revolution with social consequences,"
as Taylor put it. But another strand of revisionism, proposed
first by Eisenstein, returned to the influence of the Enlightenment, arguing that the early revolutionaries were above all
an Enlightened elite, "a loose coalition of like-minded men
drawn from all three estates." The French historian and public intellectual François Furet, who eventually became the
reigning prince of the revisionist school, would also down-
play the importance of social factors and would lay great
stress on the impact of ideas on the French Revolution. In

[20] E.g., Vivian Gruder, *The Royal Provincial Intendants* (Ithaca, 1968);
David Bien, "La réaction aristocratique avant 1789: l'exemple de l'armée,"
Annales. Economies, Sociétés, Civilisations 29 (1974): 23–48, 505–34; Daniel
Roche, *Le siècle des lumières en province*, 2 vols. (Paris, 1978); Doyle, *Ori-
gins of the French Revolution*, 197.

Furet's view the writings of Rousseau, in particular, were fundamental to the origins of both 1789 and the Terror.[21]

But beyond the revisionist onslaught against the class analysis of the French Revolution, a half century of research—much of it initially inspired by Lefebvre's work—suggests the need for a variety of other modifications and updates to *The Coming of the French Revolution*. Four directions of explicit or implicit criticism can be indicated briefly. First, Lefebvre's treatment of religion and the church now seems remarkably thin, if not dismissive. Maurice Hutt, John McManners, and others have shown how long-standing opposition between commoner parish priests and aristocratic bishops—involving both theological and pastoral issues and the distribution of church power and wealth—culminated in the parish priests' highly visible pamphlet war on the eve of the Revolution that strongly underwrote the struggle of the Third Estate against the nobility. And Dale Van Kley has argued that the battles between Jansenists and Jesuits, which unrolled over much of the century, influenced the discourse and vocabulary of the pre-Revolutionary patriot party.[22]

Second, studies over the last twenty years have brought to light Lefebvre's general neglect of the role played by women in the early phases of the Revolution. His explanation of the uprising of October 5–6 seems particularly weak in this

---

[21] Taylor, "Noncapitalist Wealth," 491; Eisenstein, "Who Intervened?" 99; François Furet, *Interpreting the Revolution*, trans. Elborg Forster (Cambridge, 1981).

[22] Maurice G. Hutt, "The Role of the Curés in the Estates General of 1789," *Journal of Ecclesiastical History* 6 (1955): 190–220; and "The Curés and the Third Estate: The Ideas of Reform in the Pamphlets of the French Lower Clergy in the Period 1787–1789," *Journal of Ecclesiastical History* 8 (1957): 74–92; John McManners, *French Ecclesiastical Society under the Ancien Régime* (Manchester, 1960); also Timothy Tackett, *Priest and Parish in Eighteenth-Century France* (Princeton, 1977); and Dale Van Kley, *The Religious Origins of the French Revolution* (New Haven, 1996).

regard. In the end, as we have seen, he largely relied on a plot theory, implying that the patriot revolutionaries consciously initiated the October Days in order to administer a "second dose of revolution" to the king. He concluded that the women's march on the 5th must have been instigated from above by male actors—even though he admitted that there was no evidence for such an influence. Yet more recent studies by George Rudé and Olwen Hufton—as well as the older study by Mathiez—seem clearly to refute the conspiracy explanation. They provide ample evidence of the spontaneity and substantial autonomy of the women's actions, actions that were central in initiating the event, even though the coercive strength of the Paris national guard, who followed the women to Versailles some six hours later, was probably more influential in forcing the king to return to Paris.[23]

Third, recent scholarship suggests a far more complex picture of what Lefebvre's student Jean Egret called the "Pre-Revolution" of 1787–1788. Both Lefebvre and Eisenstein believed that the mobilization of the Third Estate began only in the fall of 1788 with the conservative ruling of the Parlement of Paris on voting in the Estates General and with the organization in Paris of the liberal "Committee of Thirty." But evidence now places far greater emphasis on earlier political activities in the provinces, stimulated not by Parisian liberals, but by the royal government's circular letter of July 1788 soliciting advice on how the Estates General should be organized. The "Committee of Thirty" began its activities only after several weeks of intense activity in the provinces. It also seems clear that the political organization

---

[23] George Rudé, *The Crowd in the French Revolution* (Oxford, 1959); Olwen Hufton, *Women and the Limits of Citizenship in the French Revolution* (Toronto, 1992); Albert Mathiez, "Etude critique sur les journées des 5 et 6 octobre 1789," *Revue historique* 67 (1898): 241–81; 68 (1899): 258–94; 69 (1899): 41–66.

of the conservative aristocracy was by no means confined to the Assembly of Notables, as Lefebvre strongly implied. By the end of 1788, a "committee of one hundred" centered on the parlementary noble Duval d'Eprémesnil was vigorously organizing nobles throughout the kingdom in the name of a conservative political agenda and a surprisingly well defined conservative ideology. Indeed, the writings of Jean-Clément Martin and others have asserted the existence of a counter-revolution developing more or less concurrently with the Revolution itself.[24]

Finally, research over the last several decades has revised Lefebvre's interpretation of the relations between the peasantry and the nobility. It now seems clear that through June 1789 the overwhelming majority of peasant riots arose not from anger against the aristocracy, but from the problems of obtaining food in conditions of near famine. When true antiseigneurial revolts did break out in July and August—as distinguished from the panic of the Great Fear—they occurred in only seven quite limited regions of France. The rioters in question targeted not only nobles but clergymen, middle-class townsmen, royal officials, tax collectors, and even some elements of the wealthier peasantry. Moreover, renewed studies of the Great Fear underscore the widespread and continuing collaboration between the countrypeople and the nobles in the face of the panic. The belief in an "aristocratic conspiracy," which Lefebvre saw as central in 1789 to the perceptions of peasants and townsmen alike, now

[24] Jean Egret, *The French Pre-Revolution, 1787–1788* (Chicago, 1977; originally published in French in 1962); Timothy Tackett, *Becoming a Revolutionary: The Deputies of the French National Assembly and the Emergence of a Revolutionary Culture (1789–1790)* (Princeton, 1996); Jean-Clément Martin, *Contre-Révolution, Révolution, et Nation en France, 1789–1799* (Paris, 1998). On the Committee of Thirty see Daniel L. Wick, *A Conspiracy of Well-Intentioned Men: The Society of Thirty and the French Revolution* (New York, 1987).

appears to have been little in evidence outside of Paris and a few of the larger towns. Such an obsession, along with peasant antiseigneurial sentiments in general, probably arose much more gradually over the first several years of the Revolution, instigated in part—as John Markoff has suggested—by the new legislation of the various national assemblies.[25]

IV

Inevitably, then, some sixty-five years of new research have revealed both errors and omissions in George Lefebvre's interpretation of the origins of 1789. Given what we know of his commitment to a "scientific" history and his willingness to modify his views based on new evidence, it seems likely that he would have welcomed much of this new research and supported its integration into a revised synthesis on the subject. One can imagine that he might well have been persuaded to reconsider his views on the pre-Revolutionary period and on the peasantry and to have inserted an expanded treatment of women and of Old Regime religious issues. Whether he would also have been won over by the contentions of the "revisionists," however, seems more problematic. Reacting to the early critiques of Alfred Cobban, he praised the British

[25] John Markoff, *The Abolition of Feudalism: Peasants, Lords, and Legislators in the French Revolution* (University Park, Pa., 1996). See also Anatoli Ado, *Paysans en révolution. Terre, pouvoir et jacquerie, 1789–1794* (Paris, 1996); and Timothy Tackett, "La grande peur de 1789 et la thèse du complot aristocratique," *AHRF* 76 (2004): 1–17; and "Collective Panics in the Early French Revolution, 1789–1791: A Comparative Perspective," *French History* 17 (2003): 149–71. See also Peter M. Jones, "Georges Lefebvre and the Peasant Revolution: Fifty Years On," *French Historical Studies* 16 (1990): 645–63.

historian for his new quantitative analysis of the social origins of the deputies to the Estates General, but he remained
unconvinced by Cobban's broader attack on the concept of a
bourgeois revolution, and he continued to insist on the
importance of social and economic factors in the origins and
development of the Revolution.

In any case, the last decade of the twentieth century would
see the publication of a number of "revisionist" reconsidera-
tions of revisionism.[26] If Lefebvre's *longue durée* explanation
of the Revolution as the result of the struggle between two
economic classes seems less persuasive than it once did,
many scholars are unprepared to reduce the Revolution
entirely to issues of ideology and politics. The questioning of
a Marxist analysis of socioeconomic forces in the Revolution
should not prevent historians from exploring the significance
of social and economic factors more generally—very much
in the spirit of the complex and multivariate empirical analysis that marked most of Lefebvre's writing.

The Coming of the French Revolution is no longer a sum-
mation of the latest research in the field—as it certainly was
when it was first written in 1939 and first translated into
English in 1947. Nevertheless, even at the beginning of the
twenty-first century, it remains a masterpiece of narrative
and analytical concision, a powerful and extraordinarily
readable account of one of the most dramatic moments in
recent world history. It continues to impress us in its sensitive and subtle probing of collective mentality and psychology, in its ability to bring the Revolution to life, not as an
affair of logic and calculation, but as an experience of

[26] See, e.g., Bill Edmonds, "Successes and Excesses of Revisionist Writing about the French Revolution," *European Historical Quarterly* 17 (1987):
195–217; Colin Jones, "Bourgeois Revolution Revivified, 1789 and Social
Change," in *Rewriting the French Revolution*, ed. Colin Lucas (Oxford,
1991), 69–118; and Tackett, *Becoming a Revolutionary*.

intense emotion and quasi-utopian enthusiasm, intermingled with strong elements of fear and suspicion. In this sense, like the earlier works of Jules Michelet, Alexis de Tocqueville, and Jean Jaurès, it will remain one of the great classics of French Revolutionary history.

Paris
September 2004

Note to the Princeton Classic Edition

I HAVE taken advantage of this new edition to correct a handful of minor errors and inconsistencies that slipped into R. R. Palmer's otherwise superb translation. The opening section has been entitled "Prologue," rather than "Introduction," since this seems a more appropriate designation for the ideas developed within, and it also distinguishes the section more clearly from the general introduction to the edition (Lefebvre gave no title to his opening in the original French version). But the most important change has been the insertion of the final two paragraphs of Georges Lefebvre's original text, omitted by Palmer in all previous editions. I have translated the paragraphs myself from the 1939 French edition (assisted by suggestions from James Friguglietti). As I have argued above, the book has become a true classic of historical literature. In order to fully appreciate the work and the context in which it was written, it now seems essential to provide the integral of Lefebvre's text—including his final appeal to French youth, as they faced the threat of fascism in 1939, to remember the ideals of the French Revolution.

In addition, it seemed appropriate to include substantial excerpts from Palmer's most recent preface of 1988. For over forty years, Palmer, who died in 2002, closely associated himself with *Quatre-Vingt-Neuf* and its translation and subsequent editions. As he explains elsewhere, he had been substantially influenced by Lefebvre in his own historical work, most notably in his celebrated study of the Terror, *Twelve Who Ruled* (Princeton, 1941). In the excerpts reprinted here Palmer provides a personal tribute to the French historian and his interpretation. In so doing, he also gives testimony of his own understanding of the significance and achievements of the French Revolution.

Timothy Tackett

From the Translator's 1988 Preface

EVEN TODAY, toward the close of the twentieth century, despite all the revolutions, wars, and massacres that our troubled century has seen, and even in America or other parts of the world where the countries of Europe no longer exert their former influence, it is still possible to say that the French Revolution was a great turning point in the formation of the modern world.

The Revolution announced the principle of the sovereignty of the people or nation. Over a hundred and sixty such "nations" now sit in the United Nations in New York. It was also a revolution of liberty and equality, to which it added fraternity, meaning at first a national citizenship in which persons of different social classes and ethnic backgrounds could find a common ground. Reinforcing and magnifying the example set in America, the Revolutionaries in France began by drafting an explicit written constitution to create and regulate the powers of government, and they prefaced it with a Declaration of the Rights of Man and the Citizen, or what are now called human and civil rights.

Paradoxes of the modern world are found in the Revolution. The Revolution liberated the individual and consolidated the modern state. It preached democracy, and went through a phase of terror and dictatorship. At first denouncing war as a stratagem of governments, it made war more all-consuming by putting a whole nation behind its armies.

It contributed to the growth of capitalism, and it gave inspiration to socialism. It supposed all peoples to be moving at different rates in the same line of progress, and at the same time, by the resistance that it aroused, it persuaded many peoples that each nation should go its own way. And so far as the tensions of modern society result from telling all human beings that they enjoy the same rights, while in fact they do not participate equally in the good things of life, these tensions may be ascribed to the French Revolution, and they are not likely to disappear in the future. . . .

[B]oth historical and popular opinion on the French Revolution, as on any revolution, has been divided. Was the Revolution "necessary"? Or how much of it was "necessary," and at what point in its progressive course did the "excesses" begin? At one extreme is the belief that no revolution was necessary at all in 1789, either because the Old Regime was a satisfactory society, or because wiser and more statesman-like policies could have met and mastered the problems of the day without revolution. This latter view was expressed at the time by Edmund Burke, and has attracted followers ever since; but no one has ever been able to suggest positively by what means the crisis of 1789 could have been met within the limits of the prevailing regime, so that partisans of this view usually reveal themselves negatively, by dwelling on the errors and imbecilities of the original revolutionaries. At the other extreme is the view that the whole Revolution was necessary, from the Oath of the Tennis Court in June 1789 to the Great Terror of the early summer of 1794; that the whole sequence of events was a *bloc* which stands or falls together; and that each successive wave of revolutionary action, each going farther than the last, was necessary to prevent relapse into the Old Regime and loss of all gains accomplished, so that, strictly speaking, there were no "excesses." This theory too is incapable of proof, and suffers from the fact that most of the revolutionary leaders themselves did not believe it, since one group after another, each in turn concluding that the movement was going "too far," dissociated itself from it and went over to the counterrevolution, or at least to what was called counterrevolution by the newly emerging revolutionary party. Thus there are various middle grounds, in which the early phases of the Revolution are called wise and constructive, the later phases ruinous or fanatical. In general, the argument that the Revolution was necessary, wholly or in part, reveals itself in the argument of self-defense: the revolutionaries *had* to do thus and so because of the threats and provocations of their opponents. On the other hand, writers who sympathize with what may be called the relatively conservative forces in the Revolution, the king or the aristocracy in 1789, or the Girondists or Dantonists in 1793–1794, also resort to arguments of necessity and self-defense: these elements, they seem to say, *had* to rally against the uncalled-for, impolitic or unnecessary provocation of the Left.

Necessity in these contexts does not mean a necessity imposed by a superhuman determinism or indemonstrable dialectic. It is a necessity compatible with freedom of choice, a necessity flowing from judgment, purpose and policy, expressible in the formula that one must do so-and-so in order to achieve such-and-such ends. It is the familiar necessity of practical life, that one who wills an objective must will the means to attain it, or, if the means are unacceptable, change the objective. This is essentially what happened in the French Revolution: many Frenchmen in 1789 shared in similar objectives; but some, continuing to hold to the objective, "had" to adopt means which they disliked (Robespierre, for example, did not "like" the Terror), while others, unable sooner or later to accept the means, "had" to change their objective, i.e., turn against the ongoing Revolution. Differences of opinion over what was necessary turn into differences as to what objectives were legitimate. So long as one thinks it to have been wise, feasible or legitimate to try to introduce a kind of political democracy in France in the eighteenth century, one must regard as necessary, in the judgment of the present translator, virtually all the steps taken by the revolutionaries down to the dictatorship of 1793–1794. To consider these steps unnecessary, deploring them as "excesses," requires one to say that the objective of political democracy in France at the time was a false or impossible one, which should have been given up as the means used to attain it became apparent. At the far pole, in this direction, lies the doctrine of Burke, who held in effect that the wise, feasible and legitimate policy for the French in 1789 was to maintain the aristocratic class structure and established church of the day, and that the whole Revolution from the beginning was therefore an unnecessary outburst of irresponsible extremism. On the relative merits of the two polar viewpoints represented by Robespierre and Burke there can never be general agreement, nor will the same person, if judicious, always and in all moods be of exactly the same opinion. This is because the issue is a question of policy, and questions of policy are not and should not be matters of dogma.

That the Revolution was necessary Lefebvre does not doubt: the old government simply failed to function, and its officials either would not or could not take the measures necessary to maintain political life. He grants that opinion may differ on whether it was necessary for the Revolution to go so far. He holds, however, that if the desideratum was to create a regime at all democratic, avoiding an aristocratic order either like the Old Regime in France or like the regime then prevailing in England, it was probably necessary for the movement to work itself out about as it did. On the debated question of who "started" the Revolution, whose provocation it was which justified the subsequent tumult, he answers that all classes were in one way or another responsible; that the

aristocracy, the bourgeoisie, the urban masses and the peasants, each independently and for reasons of its own, initiated
revolutionary action. On the charge that the Revolution was
pushed forward by small, determined minorities, little
anonymous societies of extremists or committees of correspondence, he declares that this is in fact so, that all political
movements require leaders and that in any case such highhanded methods were first used by the aristocracy. He thus
disarms those critics, mainly upper-class Frenchmen, who
have given the impression that the Revolution was something unleashed on the nation by little bands of irresponsible middle-class radicals. On the matter of mob violence
and atrocities, Lefebvre admits freely that they occurred. He
points out that popular fury impelled statesmen onward,
and that mobs aiming at short-run material ends helped to
force acceptance of far-reaching ideas which they did not
understand. He concedes that disreputable and murderous
characters filtered into the insurgent crowds, but he does
not think that such characters affected the course of the
Revolution. He sometimes dwells on violence, but he insists
that it was by resorting to violence that the French people
freed themselves of many ancient burdens. He argues, too,
that the use of violence by the revolutionaries was fundamentally defensive, arising as early as July 1789 from fear of
an "aristocratic conspiracy" against the Third Estate.

Analysis of the composition and action of social classes
provides the basic structure of the book. Yet it is not the
struggle of classes that occupies the author, so much as their
potential fusion. Lefebvre shows how all classes combined,
under the leadership of the aristocracy, to overthrow the
absolutist Bourbon regime and demand a constitutional
order guaranteeing individual rights. Division thereafter took
place, for the aristocracy, being only human, hesitated to
surrender all the privileges of its position. The bourgeoisie
came to the fore, taking advantage of popular insurrection

in town and country. But the regime introduced by the bourgeoisie was not an instrument of class domination; it had something to offer to everybody, and indeed postulated that no such things as fixed classes existed. Within the bourgeois order, because of the liberties which it gave, could arise eventually a new order aiming at a fuller realization of social justice. This was because of the great flexibility and high level of abstraction of the philosophy of natural rights expressed in the Declaration of the Rights of Man and the Citizen, which Lefebvre analyzes at some length. It was in this way, he seems to feel, that the philosophy of the eighteenth century influenced the Revolution. The writings of Rousseau, Voltaire and others like them did not "cause" the Revolution, which arose from a perfectly definite series of concrete political events; but the Revolution, once started, expressed itself in the broad conception of eighteenth century thought, in which "man" was a fundamental reality, with all classes, nations and races of merely secondary importance. Thus the Revolution addressed itself to all men alike, as did the Christian religion; and seeing the similarity, M. Lefebvre is both firmly republican and not at all anticlerical or antireligious. In general, it is obviously a source of great pride to him that the French Revolution of 1789 knew no pariah classes, races or nations, but presented a universal philosophy in which, were it only accepted, all human beings could at least in principle live at peace, equal in dignity and treating one another as equals.

The translation published in 1947 benefited from the correction by Lefebvre of a few slight errors that had crept into the original. I remain indebted to him, since his death, for his cordial co-operation at that time. All footnotes except the one on page 88 are by me, added in the hope of assisting the English-speaking reader. I have tried to find English equivalents for French terms so far as possible, believing that the use of such terms as *gabelle, lettre de cachet,* etc., though familiar to English-speaking readers versed in the subject, may not be clear to those approaching it for the first time, and in any case that it confirms a stereotyped impression of French society in the eighteenth century, making it seem unduly distant from us today, and more unlike other societies of the past and present than seems to me to be justified.

R. R. Palmer
Princeton, N.J.
1988

THE COMING
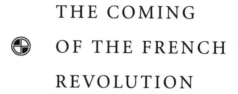 OF THE FRENCH
REVOLUTION

Prologue

THE ULTIMATE CAUSE of the
French Revolution of 1789 goes deep into the history of
France and of the western world. At the end of the eighteenth
century the social structure of France was aristocratic. It
showed the traces of having originated at a time when land
was almost the only form of wealth, and when the possessors
of land were the masters of those who needed it to work and
to live. It is true that in the course of age-old struggles (of
which the Fronde, the last revolt of the aristocracy, was as
recent as the seventeenth century) the king had been able
gradually to deprive the lords of their political power and
subject nobles and clergy to his authority. But he had left
them the first place in the social hierarchy. Still restless at
being merely his "subjects," they remained privileged persons.

Meanwhile the growth of commerce and industry had created, step by step, a new form of wealth, mobile or commercial wealth, and a new class, called in France the bourgeoisie,
which since the fourteenth century had taken its place as the
Third Estate in the General Estates of the kingdom. This class
had grown much stronger with the maritime discoveries of
the fifteenth and sixteenth centuries and the ensuing exploita-
tion of new worlds, and also because it proved highly useful
to the monarchical state in supplying it with money and com-
petent officials. In the eighteenth century commerce, industry
and finance occupied an increasingly important place in the

national economy. It was the bourgeoisie that rescued the royal treasury in moments of crisis. From its ranks were recruited most members of the liberal professions and most public employees. It had developed a new ideology which the "philosophers" and "economists" of the time had simply put into definite form. The role of the nobility had correspondingly declined; and the clergy, as the ideal which it proclaimed lost prestige, found its authority growing weaker. These groups preserved the highest rank in the legal structure of the country, but in reality economic power, personal abilities and confidence in the future had passed largely to the bourgeoisie. Such a discrepancy never lasts forever. The Revolution of 1789 restored the harmony between fact and law. This transformation spread in the nineteenth century throughout the west and then to the whole globe, and in this sense the ideas of 1789 toured the world.

But this deeper cause of the French Revolution does not explain all its distinctive features. In England, though there have been political revolutions, social evolution has gone on in relative calm. The French Revolution was realized by violence. On the Continent, in the nineteenth century, the transformation was first precipitated by the Napoleonic armies, and thereafter carried through more by governments than by the peoples themselves. In France the Third Estate liberated itself. Hence the older aristocracy long preserved more wealth and influence in other countries than in France. These special features of the Revolution in France arose from its immediate causes, and especially from the collapse of the central power which in other countries was able to keep events under control.

There would have been no French Revolution—such as actually took place—if the king, "handing in his resignation," had not convoked the Estates-General. The immediate cause lay in a government emergency for which Louis XVI could find no other solution. But the Third Estate was by no means

the first to profit from the emergency, contrary to the general
opinion, taken over from the Revolutionists themselves, who
declared *ad nauseam* that "the people rose up and overthrew
despotism and aristocracy." No doubt it did end that way. But
the people were not the original motive force. The bourgeoisie, having no legal means of expression, was in no position to force the king to appeal to the nation. Still less were the
peasants and working classes. The privileged groups did have
the necessary means: the clergy in its Assembly, the nobility in
the Parlements and Provincial Estates. It is these bodies that
forced the king's hand. "The patricians began the Revolution,"
wrote Chateaubriand; "the plebeians finished it." The first act
of the Revolution, in 1788, consisted in a triumph of the aristocracy, which, taking advantage of the government crisis,
hoped to reassert itself and win back the political authority of
which the Capetian dynasty had despoiled it. But, after having
paralyzed the royal power which upheld its own social preeminence, the aristocracy opened the way to the bourgeois revolution, then to the popular revolution in the cities and finally to
the revolution of the peasants—and found itself buried under
the ruins of the Old Regime. These four acts we shall reconstruct in their main outlines.

PART I ⊕ THE ARISTOCRATIC
REVOLUTION

CHAPTER 1   *The Aristocracy*

IN THE old France the law dis-
tinguished three *orders*: Clergy, Nobility and Third Estate.
Their numerical proportions are not definitely known, but in
a total population of probably 23,000,000 there were certainly not more than 100,000 priests, monks and nuns, and
400,000 nobles. All the rest constituted the Third Estate.

The clergy, besides its honorific preeminence, possessed
very great privileges. It was an organized body, represented
by a periodical Assembly, equipped with its own administration (agents-general of the clergy, diocesan chambers, etc.)
and provided with its own courts of law, called officialities. It
was subject to none of the ordinary direct taxes but instead
determined on its own authority a "free donation" to the
king. Sometimes it borrowed money for the use of the state,
assuming the interest and amortization charges. Materially it
depended neither on the state nor on the generosity of the
faithful. It collected the tithe on all products of the soil, and
its own landed property, very extensive in the north, somewhat less so as one went west and south, comprised probably
a tenth of the kingdom. Bishops, abbots and chapters were
lords over many villages, and as such received manorial dues.
Closely allied with the monarchy, whose divine right was
symbolized by the religious ceremony of coronation, the
clergy exercised a control over thought in the interests of
both Church and king, possessed a monopoly in education

and poor relief and shared in the censorship of everything that was lawfully printed. Since the revocation of the Edict of Nantes all Frenchmen were considered to be Catholics. Official records of birth, marriage and death were kept by the parish priests. Without Catholic sacraments the king's subject had no legal existence; his children were reputed bastards and had no rights of inheritance. Not until the beginning of 1788 did the authorities reluctantly concede the continued existence of Protestants and make exceptions in their favor.

But strictly speaking the clergy, as Sieyès said, was a profession and not a social class. Its unity was purely spiritual, representing the Church, a perfect and divine society. Socially the clergy was differentiated into nobles—especially the upper clergy, such as bishops, abbots and many canons—and commoners, who included almost all the parish priests and most persons in monastic orders. These social distinctions were to become clear at the Estates-General when the parish priests assured the victory of the Third Estate.

There were in reality, therefore, only two classes, nobles and commoners. The aristocracy meant the nobility.

The Nobles: The Interplay of Rank and Money

The nobility also enjoyed privileges, some "honorific," such as the right to carry the sword, others "useful," such as exemption from the tax known as the *taille* and from obligations for road service and quartering troops; but it was less favored than the clergy, not forming an organized body and being subject to the poll-tax and the twentieth-taxes.[1] The nobles still owned considerable land,

---

[1] The *taille* (the word originally meant the "cut" taken by the lord from the subject) was the basic tax of the French monarchy before the Revolution. It varied in both form and burdensomeness from province to

probably a fifth of the territory of the kingdom, and they possessed the majority of the manors and hence the right to receive feudal dues. But these facts established no radical distinction between them and commoners. Privileges were enjoyed also by provinces, cities and government officials

---

province, and was never paid by anyone who because of class status, regional privilege or personal influence could obtain exemption, so that not to be *taillable* was one of the most common of privileges, and to be *taillable* was not only a financial expense but a social indignity. In general, the *taille* was paid only by the poor, especially the peasants. There were two additional modern direct taxes, payable in principle by all: (1) the *capitation*, inadequately translated as "poll-tax" because unlike the poll-tax as understood in America it was levied in rough correspondence to income; and (2) the *vingtième* or "twentieth," originally conceived as a kind of 5 per cent tax on income; but influential groups—Church, nobility, provinces and certain corporate organizations of the bourgeoisie—had so successfully watered down these obligations (by compounding once and for all through paying a lump sum, by concealing the true amount of income or by other means) that these two taxes also were undermined by privilege, unjust in their incidence and insufficiently remunerative to the government. Also to be considered as direct taxes, though paid in service rather than in money, were the *corvées royales* consisting in (a) the *transports militaires*, by which civilians lent the use of carts, etc., to assist in troop movements, and above all (b) the *corvée des routes*, by which people within five or ten miles of the through highways or *routes royales* were called upon to supply labor, teams and wagons to keep them in repair, usually being liable for from six to thirty days a year. Only peasants were subject to these *corvées*, though of course it was not mainly the peasants who benefited. Commutation of *corvées* into a money tax was often considered by government administrators during the eighteenth century, but never generally or successfully introduced.

The difficulty of the Bourbon monarchy in levying direct taxes arose from a fundamental weakness in the absolutist structure, viz., that the government ruled without the express consent of influential groups within the country. The king's government, unwilling or unable to allow participation of these groups in the formation of policy, persuaded them to accept its authority by assuring them "liberties," such as immunities to taxation. Contrariwise, the influential groups—Church, nobility,

who were not nobles. Many bourgeois did not pay the *taille*. Peasants were the only persons subject to drawing lots for militia service and to statute labor on the roads. In France it was not prohibited, as it was in Prussia, for bourgeois and peasants to acquire land and even manors, and they did so without backwardness or embarrassment.

What really characterized the nobility was birth; it was possible to become a noble, but in the eyes of everyone the true nobleman was born. It was from blood that the noble derived his superiority over the "ignoble" commoners, and hence it followed that noble status was inalienable and that

---

privileged provinces, etc.—took the position that if they were not represented in the government they were under no obligation to pay taxes to it. The tax exemptions of the Old Regime thus reflect, inversely, the well-known American principle of "no taxation without representation." The result was that most direct taxes were paid by persons lacking the status or influence to bargain with the king's officials, and that the king's government could never raise by direct taxes a revenue at all proportionate to the real wealth of the country, or to its legitimate needs.

Hence the monarchy resorted heavily to indirect taxes, which in principle were paid by all classes, but which in effect, since they fell on articles of common consumption, were borne mainly by the least wealthy. Indirect taxes included (1) the customs duties, including internal customs duties; (2) the excises or *aides* on wines, liquors, playing cards, soap, etc., and (3) the government monopolies of tobacco, salt, etc., especially the salt monopoly or *gabelle*, by which the government required its subjects to purchase fixed amounts of salt at a figure far higher than the economic price. Some privileged provinces were wholly or partly exempt from the *gabelle*. The indirect taxes were "farmed," i.e., collected by the private enterprise of concessionaires who made tax-farming a business. There were two general reasons for the farming system: an administrative reason, in that the central government lacked the machinery for dealing with millions of individuals on small matters; and a financial reason, in that the government, always hard-pressed for cash, obtained an immediate lump sum from the farmers, leaving them the right to make a profit by collecting over a period of time the whole amount legally due.

an unsuitable marriage was an ineffaceable blot. The aristocratic literature that flourished in the eighteenth century,
more than is generally realized, side by side with the bourgeois philosophy, set itself to fortify this racial phantas-
magoria by imaginary portrayals of French social history.
To the comte de Boulainvilliers the nobles were descen-
dants of the early Germans who had established themselves
by conquest as lords over the persons and lands of the
Gallo-Romans, conceived to be unskillful in arms and timid
in the face of death. They were a distinct race, heroic and
military, made for command and insistent upon the marks
of respect assured by honorific distinctions. How could
such men dream of being confounded with the rest of the
nation?

The noble "derogated" or fell into the common mass if he
followed a business or profession. Colbert had permitted
nobles to engage in maritime commerce, but with only
moderate success. Unless very poor, the noble did not even
manage his own property. From idleness he often saw his
fortune slip away. War no longer paid; hence younger sons
tried to establish their claims despite primogeniture. The
cost of living in the eighteenth century had greatly risen.
The nobility as a class was less and less homogeneous. Some
were very rich, like La Fayette, who inherited 140,000 livres a
year at the death of his father.[2] They lived at court or in
sumptuous chateaux, like Rohan at Saverne and Brienne at
Brunoy. Their manner of life often lacked balance and seri-
ousness, and many ended up greatly in debt, for example the
Guéménée family, which went bankrupt on the eve of the

---

[2] The livre, renamed the franc during the Revolution, was the basic cur-
rency unit. It consisted of 20 sous, and 24 livres made up a louis d'or, a
gold coin of about the value of an English guinea. An income of 140,000
livres would be equal to about 7,000 English pounds sterling. A skilled
worker's family might live on 1,000 livres a year if regularly employed.

Revolution. The provincial nobles led a less dissipated existence; many were scarcely comfortable and some were even poor, especially in the hilly regions. The large class of needy gentry were of all the nobility the most wedded to tradition and the least inclined to concessions, for they feared that to give up their feudal rights or even to pay more taxes would consummate their ruin.

Alongside this nobility of the sword, the old nobility or nobility that called itself such, another nobility had arisen. The king could create nobles, and had not failed to reward his servants in this manner. Having formed the habit, to obtain money, of putting up public offices for sale, especially judgeships but also financial, military, administrative and municipal offices, the kings had reached the point in the sixteenth and seventeenth centuries of conferring nobility on some of these employments in order to increase the price. Hereditary noble status was granted to members of the Paris law courts—the Parlement, Court of Accounts, Court of Aids, Great Council, Court of Coinage—and of some courts in the provinces. In other cases noble status was conceded only as a personal right but became transmissible to heirs after a certain number of years. This was known as nobility of the robe. Similar favors were accorded to the masters of petitions of the king's council, to officials in the bureaus of finance and general tax collectors, to secretaries of the king who were dispersed in numbers running to several hundreds throughout the kingdom without having any function, to the mayors and magistrates of certain towns. These nobles, of recent bourgeois extraction, were wealthy because their offices had a high market value and because ordinarily, through family tradition, they knew how to administer and augment their inheritances. The nobility of the sword long held them in some contempt, but in the eighteenth century this feeling was lessened, for the lure of dowries brought on marriages that hastened assimilation, and in any case the

new nobles soon forgot their origins and were no less proud
than the old.

The nobility had become greatly dependent on money,
without which the future was closed. The time was no longer
when the youngster from Gascony came to seek his fortune at
court, for the impoverished nobleman could no longer serve
there. Even in the army promotion for him was closely
restricted, for a regiment cost from 25,000 to 50,000 livres.
Hence many were hunters of sinecures, pensions or outright
gifts if they could only get close to the king, or at least rich
marriages, even at the price of somewhat degrading connections. Choiseul married the daughter of Crozat, Molé the
daughter of Bernard, the bride's father in both cases being
famous and wealthy from farming the government revenues.
A daughter of the banker Laborde became the comtesse de
Noailles. A more interesting fact is that the nobles let themselves be won over by the bourgeois spirit, took an interest in
the progress of capitalism and tried to obtain some of its profits through using their influence with the administration or
invoking their feudal rights. The manorial lords long claimed
the right to grant mining concessions for properties on their
estates. In 1744 the king made mining concessions dependent
on the Crown, but in any case the nobles were favorably placed
to obtain them, and the duc de Croy, for example, played an
important part in the formation of the Anzin coal interests.
Timber and water rights for the most part belonged to the
manorial domains; they were indispensable in the eighteenth
century to iron-smelting and glass-making, as well as other
types of manufacture. Some noblemen invested in industry.
The comte d'Artois had stock in the Javel works, and Buffon
set up an iron foundry at Montbard. Others speculated in real
estate. The duc d'Orléans built apartment houses at the Palais-
Royal. Some bought shares in the Tax Concession which
collected the customs duties and managed the sale of salt,
which was a government monopoly; or joined in companies

supplying the army and navy; or speculated on the Stock Exchange. The abbé d'Espagnac and Talleyrand were already known before the Revolution for their operations on the Exchange.

More traditionally minded, some great landowners tried to raise their incomes by developing their estates according to methods advocated by the Physiocrats and imitated from England. Among these were the marquis de Turbilly at Volandry in Touraine, the duc de La Rochefoucauld at Liancourt, Montlosier at Randanne near Clermont, Lavoisier in the Blésois. But most lords confined themselves to demanding their feudal rights with a new rigor, a turn of events often called the feudal reaction. They farmed out their rights to bourgeois agents who were relentless in collection of dues; they had minutely detailed manor-rolls drawn up, putting into effect dues which had become obsolete; they prevailed upon the king to issue edicts allowing them to appropriate a third of the common lands or to enclose their own fields and forbid the peasants to pasture their animals in them; they made use of the "planting right" to set out trees along the roads on land belonging to the peasants; they expelled the peasants from the forests.

These consequences of the race for money were emphasized by Tocqueville. At its upper level the nobility tended to suffer amputation of a minority whose conditions of life drew them to the bourgeoisie and gave them liberal ideas. These were envious of the English lords who enriched themselves in bourgeois ways and who by sitting in Parliament formed the ministry and government of the country. At its lower level the nobility also suffered from attrition. For want of money some unclassed themselves, like Mirabeau. Many younger sons dreamed of a new order in which they should have their place, or at the least, disgusted with their humdrum life, longed for adventure and exclaimed like Chateaubriand, "Arise, ye desired storms!"

The Resurgence of Aristocracy in the Eighteenth Century

Still, one should not exagger-
ate the importance of this development. The great majority
of nobles either did not know how, or did not wish, to get
rich. The great majority of younger sons had no desire to
"derogate." They sought the remedy elsewhere, in a growing
exclusiveness. Some held that the nobility should form a
body like the clergy and be constituted as a closed caste. For
the last time, in stating grievances in 1789,[3] they were to
demand a verification of titles of nobility and the suppression of automatic creation of nobility through the sale of
offices. Likewise it was held that, if the king was to count on
"his loyal nobility," he should recognize that they alone had
the necessary rank to advise him and to command in his
name; he should grant them a monopoly of employments
compatible with their dignity, together with free education
for their sons. The nobles had already obtained considerable
satisfaction in the course of the eighteenth century. The king,
first gentleman of the kingdom, had increasingly let the prerogatives of blood prevail, at the risk of thereby betraying
what may be called his national mission, and of seeing the
aristocracy turn against him the influence which he allowed
it to win.

The history of the Capetian monarchy had in fact been
largely the story of its struggle against the aristocracy. Sometimes the royal power had won out, as under Francis I and
Henry II, to go back no farther, or under Henry IV and
Richelieu. Sometimes the aristocracy had regained the
advantage, through the wars of religion, the minority of

---

[3] The reference is to the *cahiers de doléances,* or grievance-lists, prepared at the time of the elections to the Estates-General in 1789. In these
cahiers each "order" in each electoral district stated its grievances and recommended new policies to the king. See below, pages 34–36 and 71–74.

Louis XIII or the Fronde. Under Louis XIV the conflict seemed to be over, and the nobility saw itself at last even subjected to direct taxation. While consolidating the territories of France the royal power thus prepared the unity of the nation, taking local administration away from the territorial aristocracy, fighting against particularism and endeavoring to unite all Frenchmen under the same law. The Crown, in obliging clergy and nobles to obey it, put them on the same footing with the rest of the nation, at least in this respect and pending further developments in the same direction. But the successors of Louis XIV did not finish the great work. It is customary to characterize the eighteenth century as the age of the rise of the bourgeoisie and the triumph of "philosophy," but the century also witnessed the last offensive of the aristocracy, of which the beginnings of the Revolution were merely the crowning effort.

No one could complain of Louis XVI, as Saint-Simon had complained of Louis XIV, that the monarch surrounded himself with nothing but "vile bourgeoisie." Except for Necker all of Louis XVI's ministers were nobles. So were the members of his councils. To the nobles also were reserved, it need hardly be said, all the dignities of the households of the king, the queen and the princes. After every war it was the officers of common birth who were retired first. The comte de Saint-Germain, when minister of war, ruled that each time a commission changed hands its price should be reduced by a fourth; the purpose was to open the army to men of birth rather than money. After 1781 four quarterings of nobility were required to obtain a commission without passing through the ranks. In the navy, where commissions were not sold, aristocratic exclusiveness met with still fewer obstacles. All the bishops were noblemen in 1789. The Parlements fought against the admission of commoners and some of them openly required nobility on the father's side.[4] In any case few new offices were being created and the old ones had become virtually hereditary. Even the intendancies[5] had been encroached upon, for whereas in the time of Richelieu and Colbert the intendants had been commoners or very newly made nobles, under Louis XVI they were nobles with quarterings, who had long resided in their districts, married there, bought land and fraternized with the lords of the neighborhood. Would they not hesitate, if the struggle became acute, between the king whom they represented and the aristocracy of which they were members?

This struggle had in fact been resumed ever since the death of Louis XIV. It was no longer a question of recourse to arms. Times had changed. It was now in the field of judicature and administration, by bourgeois methods, that the Parlements or sovereign law courts, together with the Provincial Estates, held in check and undermined the royal power. The courts were courts of law, but two of their functions gave them a political role. An edict of the king was not valid in their eyes until they had registered it, and before registering it they were permitted to present remonstrances. Of course the king could take further action; he could command registration of an edict in a solemn session called a *lit de justice*. But on various

[4] For the *parlements*, of which there were thirteen in 1789, see the following paragraph. Various of the great provinces had made autonomy of their own legal systems a condition of coming under the French crown; each Parlement was the supreme or "sovereign" court of appeal in a region having its own laws and courts. Above the thirteen Parlements there was no legal authority except the king himself, though the Parlement of Paris often exerted a leadership over the others.

[5] France in 1789 was divided into thirty-four *généralités*, each in charge of an official called an *intendant*, who exercised all the king's administrative power and a good deal of his judicial power in the district; originally it had been one of the main duties of the intendants to control the local aristocracy, and they had therefore at first been men unconnected with the aristocracy or with the territory to which they were assigned.

occasions during the eighteenth century the Parlements had boldly declared such proceedings null and void, and, when the king stood his ground, had simply suspended the work of the courts. They would thereupon be exiled to another city by administrative orders (the famous *lettres de cachet*), but even so, until some compromise was reached, the original edict would remain unenforceable at law. The courts were especially troublesome when fiscal questions were at stake; under pretense of defending the taxpayer they blocked reforms aimed at the limitation of privileges. In 1774 Maupeou had broken this judicial oligarchy, but one of the first acts of Louis XVI was to reestablish it. Soon afterwards it contributed powerfully to the fall of Turgot.

The development of the Provincial Estates is less well known but no less characteristic. Louis XIV had allowed these representative assemblies to remain alive in a number of provinces. They existed in Burgundy, in Artois, Flanders and Cambrésis, in Béarn and some of the smaller districts in the Pyrenees, and in somewhat restricted form in Provence. But the most powerful of the Provincial Estates were those of Brittany and Languedoc. Here the nobility and clergy reigned supreme, and the Third Estate was represented by delegates of municipalities who were themselves nobles or at least privileged persons. In Languedoc the Third Estate had as many deputies as the first two orders combined and voting was not by order but by individual member, yet the interests of the aristocracy did not suffer.

Localism flourished in the Provincial Estates and the provincial courts. The estates, possessing the right of consenting to taxation, boasted like the Parlements of protecting the population against the demands of the Treasury; but they in fact used their powers to protect their own privileges and to win little by little a large share in the administration. Languedoc opened the way, Brittany followed, and in 1788 the intendant in Brittany had no powers left except over the mounted constabulary, inland transports and the supervision of beggars. The provinces which had estates aroused the envy of those which had none, and the intendants, knowing themselves to be unpopular, were increasingly cautious in exercising their powers.

In short, the nobility, not content with monopolizing the higher public employments, nourished an ambition to share in the central government and to take over all local administration. The Parlements represented themselves as the heirs of those ancient "fields of March" and "fields of May" where Frankish kings had consulted with their chief retainers, or of the *cour-le-roi* in which the early Capetians had met with their great vassals. Recalling that taxes had once been voted by the General Estates of the kingdom, the Parlements asserted that, in the absence of the national estates, this right had reverted to themselves. The aristocratic literature declared that the lords had received, with their fiefs, a sovereign power over the peasants of which the king had unjustly despoiled them. Montesquieu took up all these arguments, not excepting the theory of the Germanic origin of the nobility, in order to legitimatize the existence of the "bodies" which he believed necessary to prevent monarchy from turning into despotism; the liberty which he preached was a liberty of the aristocracy, and his *Spirit of Laws*, from this point of view, can be considered the handbook of aristocratic belief. Some writers have tried to distinguish between the nobility of the sword and the nobility of the robe, and to blame the weakening of royal power in the eighteenth century on the nobles of the robe only, seeing in them undisciplined public servants. Undoubtedly the nobility of the robe had interests of its own, for example the proprietary right to offices, which Montesquieu defended; but the nobility of the sword, though always jealous of the newer nobility of the robe, no longer regarded it as an enemy and made common cause with it against the central power. Every crisis saw cooperation between the Provincial Estates dominated by the older nobility and the Parlements which were the stronghold of the new.

Fearing both segments of the nobility, the monarchy had been unable to complete the unity of the nation. Toward national unity there had indeed been great progress, without which the Revolution would have been impossible. A thousand ties had been woven among Frenchmen by the development of communications and commerce, by the education given in the colleges, by the attraction of the court and of Paris. But provinces and towns retained their privileges. The South kept its Roman Law and the North its different regions of common law. Weights and measures were not uniform. Private tolls and internal tariffs remained. The boundaries of administrative, judicial, financial and ecclesiastical districts overlapped each other in chaos. Finally and above all, the nobility was still a nation within the nation.

The day came when a new financial crisis convinced Calonne, minister to Louis XVI, that the state must be modernized. The everlasting adversary barred the way.

CHAPTER 2　　　　*The Crisis*
of the Monarchy

THE government crisis went
back to the American war. The revolt of the English colonies
may in fact be considered the principal direct cause of the
French Revolution, both because in invoking the rights of
man it stirred up great excitement in France, and because
Louis XVI in supporting it got his finances into very bad
condition. Necker carried on the war by loans. When peace
was restored in 1783 the increase of taxes could not make up
the deficit, so that his successor Calonne continued to bor-
row. When lenders showed themselves recalcitrant, in 1786,
Calonne was obliged to notify the king that fiscal reform
was absolutely inevitable.

The Financial Impasse

For the state of the public fi-
nances Necker and Calonne blamed each other, each offering
figures which cannot now be checked. But we can form an
approximate idea from the report presented to the king in
March 1788, which consisted in a forecast of revenues and
expenses, i.e., a budget, the first of the Old Regime—and the
last. Expenses were set down at 629,000,000 livres and
revenues at 503,000,000, leaving a deficit of 126,000,000, or

20 per cent of expenses, which it was now proposed should be made up by another recourse to borrowing. Unfortunately we do not know what the actual revenues and expenditures proved to be, but the deficit must have been larger than anticipated because an economic crisis during the year, while reducing revenue, augmented expense, grain having to be purchased abroad by the state. Moreover the loan was only partially subscribed. On October 13, 1787, payment of pensions had to be partly suspended. On August 18, 1788, to enable the Bank of Discount to advance a hundred millions to the state, the government ordered acceptance of its notes as legal tender, a procedure which amounted to inflation; even so, interest and pension payments were made only after calculated delay.

Contemporaries ascribed the trouble to the shameless waste of the ministers and the Court, to the monstrous profits of the private concessionaires who collected the indirect taxes and to similar profits made by the innumerable official collectors who channeled the direct taxes into the Treasury. On this matter the privileged groups joined in chorus with the Third Estate. The grievances of all classes, as formulated in 1789, were unanimous in demanding the vote of taxes by the Estates-General and the collection of taxes by elected officials. That abuses existed is certain. Despite significant economies recently ordered, the budget of 1788 still carried the expenses of the court at 35,000,000. But this sum, considerable though it was, constituted only 6 per cent of the budget, other civil expenses accounting for 19 per cent, war, navy and diplomacy for 26 per cent. It was the debt that was crushing the royal finances, for debt service required 318,000,000, or more than 50 per cent of expenditures. New economies were not impossible; for example, there were too many officers in the army, and certain pensions could be explained by favoritism alone. But it is clear that 126,000,000 could not be saved except by reduction of the debt, that is, by repudiation. It would not have been the first repudiation in France, and since the Paris bourgeoisie would have been the victim the provincial nobility would not have especially opposed it. But the Parlements would have denounced it with vigor and the financial class would have refused any further assistance to the Treasury. The monarchy deserves credit for rejecting this expedient, and for not going further in an inflation which would have been repudiation in disguise. At the same time we should note that its attitude showed the great influence already enjoyed by the bourgeoisie.

Nor was there any hope of making up the deficit by raising existing taxes, which were already too heavy. Between the two periods 1726–1741 and 1785–1789 it appears that prices had risen 65 per cent and wages only 22 per cent. The purchasing power of the masses having diminished, taxation, especially indirect taxation, could yield no more.

There remained only one resource, though a considerable one. Not all Frenchmen paid taxes on the same basis. For one thing the regions that had retained their Provincial Estates, notably Brittany and Languedoc, bore a lighter burden. Many bourgeois did not pay the *taille* and the road service fell only on peasants. Most favored of all were the clergy and nobility. The tax exemptions from which they benefited were the more important since rural rents had risen far more than prices—98 per cent compared with 65 per cent. At the same time the value of income received in kind, as from the tithe and some feudal dues, had risen in direct proportion to prices. In short, under the Old Regime the richer a man was, the less he paid. Technically the crisis was easy to meet: all that was necessary was to make everybody pay.

Taxation and Representation—for Whom?

Calonne knew this very well. In a memorandum for the king dated August 20, 1786, he proposed to introduce the salt and tobacco monopolies into the exempted provinces, and to make the salt tax, which varied enormously from one region to another, uniform throughout. He proposed also to replace the twentieth-taxes with a "territorial subvention" to be paid by all owners of land without distinction or exception. In this way he expected not only to balance receipts and expenses, but to be able to abandon a number of special imposts, notably those on the manufacture of ironware and oils and on the transportation of ironware, oils, brandies and colonial produce. The peasants were to be relieved by commutation of the road service into money payments. By these measures Calonne hoped to stimulate economic activity and increase the taxable wealth. With this same end in view he wished to do away with the internal tariffs and grant complete freedom to the grain trade. Such a program revealed a concern for increasing wealth in harmony with the views of the economists and the bourgeoisie. By threatening the tax privileges, it aimed a blow at the social structure of the Old Regime. But Calonne went even beyond this. Foreseeing that the clergy, to excuse itself from paying the subvention, would point to the burden of debt which it had incurred for use of the state, he intended to liquidate this debt by selling the manorial properties possessed by the Church. He wished also to entrust the allocation of the tax burden to newly formed provincial assemblies, which were to be elected by landowners without distinction as to the three orders, and of which the presiding officer in each case might be a commoner.[6]

By this plan the royal power would be modernized and strengthened. If a budgetary balance could be restored, and maintained through the growth of national wealth, there

---

[6] "Allocation" of direct taxes meant the distribution among individual taxpayers of a total amount set by the government for a given region; such local "allocation" was common in the eighteenth century. Calonne's plan made the method uniform for the whole country and dependent on elected representatives of the taxpayers.

would be no more need of erratic fiscal expedients and the king would escape from the control of the Parlements. The unity of the kingdom would be greatly advanced, as would its social evolution, for the tax privileges would be reduced, a beginning would be made of extinguishing the manorial rights and all landowners, including bourgeois and peasants, would be associated in the administration and integrated into the state.

The sacrifice asked of the privileged classes was modest, for the nobility would remain exempt from the *taille*, the clergy from the poll-tax and both from the cost of maintaining the roads. But Calonne was under no illusion as to the welcome to be expected for his proposals from the Parlements. Had he been able to count on the king, perhaps he would have challenged them openly, as certain of his colleagues advised. But Louis XVI, though jealous of his authority, was lacking in will; honest and well-intentioned, he was far from being a great mind, and understood neither the dangers he was running nor the implications of his minister's plan. Moreover, although royalty as the symbol of the national community enjoyed a prestige still unimpaired, Louis XVI personally had none. Addicted to hunting and to manual hobbies, a great eater and drinker, having no fondness for society, amusements or balls, he was the laughing-stock of his courtiers. Rumors concerning the queen had made him ridiculous. His own children were said to be not his own. Marie Antoinette passed for a Messalina, and the affair of the diamond necklace in 1785 finished her reputation in the eyes of the whole nation. Among the immediate causes of the Revolution the character of the king and queen must be included. It is scarcely doubtful that events would have taken a different turn if the throne had been occupied by a Henry IV or even a Louis XIV.

Calonne resigned himself to indirect tactics. He conceived the idea of calling an assembly of notables, consisting of various elements of the nobility: fourteen prelates, thirty-six great lords, thirty-three members of Parlements, thirteen intendants and councilors of state, thirty-seven members of provincial estates and urban municipalities. Having selected them himself, and counting on administrative influence and the respect due the king, he supposed that they would be docile and that their acquiescence in his policies would make an impression on the Parlements. At bottom this was the first capitulation. The king was consulting the aristocracy instead of notifying it of his will.

Unfortunately Calonne fell ill and Vergennes, his firmest supporter in the government, had just died. The opening of the new assembly had to be put off until February 22, 1787. Meanwhile the public ridiculed the assemblage of dignitaries, while the notables themselves greatly relished their self-importance. Calonne managed to alienate them in the first meeting by revolutionary language in denouncing the abuses, which he declared the king was irrevocably determined to reform. Several of his projects, indeed, such as the commutation of road work and the reform of indirect taxes, could cause no disadvantage to the privileged groups. The assembly in fact proposed the suppression pure and simple of the salt monopoly, and its members, being landowners, stood to profit from liberation of the grain trade. But when the issue of "structural reforms" was raised, the battle began. If the clergy lost its manorial rights would not the turn of the lay lords soon follow? The rights of property were invoked. Was it not an illusion to create provincial assemblies and grant them merely the allocation of taxes? And if they were elected without regard to the three orders, would not the orders themselves perhaps one day disappear? As for the "territorial subvention," the prelates roundly attacked it as an unlimited, universal and perpetual tax, boldly recalling that the Estates-General had never approved any tax once and for all, and demanding that such a subvention be made to meet the deficit and no more. They insisted on seeing the accounts of the Treasury. There was much argument for the old system by which Provincial Estates had the right to approve of taxation and to obtain, by "subscription," the right to contribute a fixed amount which they procured by such means as they chose. Finally, the collection of a tax in kind was unanimously denounced. Later writers have wondered whether these various objections did not hide a wish to safeguard the privileges. The fact seems to be that the notables were resigned to making sacrifices. But the deficit, which put the government at such a disadvantage that Mirabeau was soon to call it the nation's treasure, was for the moment the treasure of the aristocracy. The aristocracy was willing to promise a subvention in return for political concessions, namely, the examination of accounts, i.e., a right to control the central power, and the transfer of local administration to provincial assemblies in which the aristocracy would be master.

When Calonne, with incredible self-assurance, on March 12 expressed his thanks to the notables, blandly observing that they were in agreement with him, they poured out their feelings in vehement protestations. They published a manifesto in which they conceded that the tax burden on themselves should be the same as on all other citizens, providing that "the two first orders should be preserved in the ancient forms which distinguish them." Political pamphleteers came to their support. Calonne maintained that Necker, contrary to his own statements, had left a deficit at the Treasury in 1781. Necker, who had many supporters among the notables, vainly demanded a chance to reply. Concluding that Calonne would gain nothing from the notables, the king dismissed him on April 8, 1787.

Most prominent among his opponents was Loménie de Brienne, Archbishop of Toulouse, not that at bottom he disapproved of the reforms, as was soon made clear, but that he wished to be minister, which he became at once. Considered a good administrator, Brienne was in fact an incompetent ignoramus, and he soon lost all standing by having himself transferred to the archbishopric of Sens, which was much richer. To mollify the notables he turned over the accounts, promised economies and declared himself willing to restore the three orders in the provincial assemblies and to leave the manorial rights of the clergy untouched. On the matter of the subvention he took up the counterproposal which he had used against Calonne: monetary payment and right of subscription for the provinces. But he demanded acceptance of the subvention on principle, and also of a steep increase in the stamp tax. The great majority of the notables persisted in their refusal, and even announced that they had no authority to consent to taxes, thus alluding pointedly to the Estates-General. On May 25 they were dissolved. Calonne's expedient had failed, and Brienne had now to confront the Parlements directly.

The Parlement of Paris made no trouble over registering the freedom of the grain trade, the commutation of the road service and the creation of provincial assemblies. But on the stamp tax it remonstrated, and when Brienne submitted to it the territorial subvention it refused its approval, declaring, openly this time, that only the Estates-General had authority to vote new taxes. On August 6 came a *lit de justice*, which the Parlement immediately pronounced null and void, at the same time instituting proceedings against Calonne, who fled to England. On August 14 the magistrates were exiled to Troyes. The other sovereign courts supported them in a general wave of insurgency. This was easily put down, but Brienne lost no time in capitulating. The fiscal edicts were withdrawn, and on September 19 the Parlement of Paris, reinstated in its functions, registered the restoration of the old twentieth-taxes. The government had lost a year and now stood just where it had stood before.

Since meanwhile the government had to live, Brienne like Calonne resorted to borrowing. The difficulty was still the same: he needed the consent of the Parlement, whose most influential members, disposed to bargain, did not hesitate to stipulate the decisive condition: the government must promise the calling of the Estates-General. Brienne decided to ask for 120,000,000 livres to be raised over five years, at the end of which period, in 1792, the Estates-General should be convoked. Being uncertain of a majority, he resolved to have the edict submitted to the Parlement by the king himself in a "royal session." Under this procedure, which was essentially a *lit de justice*, members of the Parlement might state their views but not proceed to a vote. To prevent concerted action the session was announced on November 18 for the following day, but that very evening the duc d'Orléans took it upon himself to speak for the opposition. When the king ordered registration the duke protested, "Sire, it is illegal!" Disconcerted, Louis XVI lost his temper, crying, "That makes no difference! It is legal because I wish it." The king's departure was followed by a tumult in which the registration was declared null and void. The duke and two councilors were exiled on the next day.

The dispute continued, the Parlement multiplying its protests, the king brushing them aside. The scope of the debate grew wilder. On January 4, 1788, the Parlement, taking up the cause of its exiled members, condemned administrative arrest and demanded individual liberty as a natural right of subjects of the king. On May 3, secretly warned that force was to be used against it, it published a declaration of the fundamental laws of the kingdom, of which it announced itself to be the custodian: that the monarchy was hereditary; that the vote of taxes was a power of the Estates-General; that Frenchmen could be judged only by ordinary magistrates who were irremovable and could not be arrested or detained arbitrarily; and finally that the customs and privileges of the provinces were inviolable. Thus the aristocracy invoked the rights of man and of citizenship to protect its members and to obtain a sharing of power with the king. On April 17 Louis XVI observed that if the Parlements had their way France would be "an aristocracy of magistrates"; he might more accurately have simply said "an aristocracy." The rumor now began to be heard that there was an Orleanist faction whose object could only be to replace Louis XVI, if it could force him to abdicate.

The government finally decided to use the extreme measures which Calonne had tried to avoid. Orders were given to arrest Duval d'Eprémesnil and Goislart de Montsabert, who had been among the boldest of the Parlement. Soldiers surrounded the Palais de Justice on May 5 and allowed no one to leave until, at six o'clock in the morning, the two leaders gave themselves up. Then on the eighth the king obtained registration for six edicts prepared by Lamoignon, the keeper of the seals. The power of registering royal edicts was transferred to a new Plenary Court, composed for the most part of princes and officers of the Crown. This was the main point. A judicial reform was added, the old judicial districts known as "bailiwicks" and "seneschalries" disappearing, and the "presidial" courts becoming courts of first instance, over which were placed appellate courts called "superior bailiwicks," so that the Parlements lost most of their jurisdiction. Torture of the type that preceded the execution of criminals was tentatively suppressed (the torture used to extract evidence having already been suppressed in 1780). Nevertheless, Lamoignon did not dare to imitate Maupeou all the way. Judges continued to enjoy both the property rights and the monetary perquisites of their offices, though both were disliked by the old nobility and by the bourgeoisie. On the other hand Lamoignon increased the authority of the royal courts over the manorial courts, granting to the former the power to hear any case brought to them by a litigant from

the latter. This was a bold infringement on judicial prerogatives regarded as essential by the manorial lords. Certain
preliminary clauses of the edicts also condemned the multi-
plicity of legal systems, so that it was thought that the central government, in depriving the several Parlements of their
right of registration, actually aimed at subverting provincial
autonomy. Like Calonne, Lamoignon had done either too
much or too little.

The Revolt of the Nobles

This time the resistance was
far more general and more violent. In Paris the Parlement
was put at once on vacation and hence condemned to
silence, but the other sovereign courts and the Châtelet took
its part, and in the provinces the Parlements and most of the
subordinate courts protested with vehemence. Peers and
dukes followed suit. The Assembly of the Clergy, which met in
June, strongly condemned the establishment of the Plenary
Court, demanded that provincial autonomy be expressly confirmed and limited itself to a "free donation" of very moderate size.[7] Nor was this the worst. As always there were popular
demonstrations in favor of the magistrates, and riots spread.
In Paris matters were kept under control. But in Toulouse the
new "superior bailiwick" had to flee. At Dijon the mounted
constabulary had to charge. At Pau on June 19, after the
mountain people had descended into the city, the intendant
was obliged to reinstate the Parlement. At Rennes the Parlement and the Provincial Estates came together to send a
deputation to Versailles. At Grenoble on June 7, as the exiled

---

[7] The "free donation" granted in 1788 amounted to 1,800,000 livres, in
contrast with an average of over 12,000,000 for the preceding twenty
Assemblies of the Clergy.

Parlement was leaving the city, the population rose up and showered the garrison with missiles from the roof tops—it was called the "Day of Tiles."

Similarly, the experiment with provincial assemblies proved a bitter one for Brienne. To please the aristocracy he had endowed them with wide powers, to the disadvantage of the intendants, and had had them meet in three separate orders with the presidency in the hands of the privileged groups. In place of elections he had himself named half the members, authorizing them to complete their numbers by cooptation, so that of 341 members representing the Third Estate 63 were nobles and 100 were privileged persons, not counting bourgeois who possessed manors or lawyers who made a living by acting as agents for manorial lords. Still the aristocracy was dissatisfied, because Brienne, imitating the Estates of Langue-doc, had granted double representation to the Third Estate and ruled that voting should be by head. The Parlement of Bordeaux forbade the meeting of the assembly of Limousin. It was "exiled." Dauphiny, Franche Comté, Hainaut and Provence demanded back their old Provincial Estates. Brienne granted the request for Provence but refused it for Dauphiny. The aristocracy of Dauphiny got out of hand and obtained the support of the bourgeoisie. This resulted in the meeting, on July 21, 1788, at Vizille, in the château of Claude Périer, despite the king's prohibition, of an assembly which called together the Provincial Estates and whose actions Brienne had to confirm.

In such circumstances it was chimerical to expect to float a loan. For want of money the French government had to let the Prussians intervene in Holland in support of the Stadholder against the Dutch bourgeoisie; the Stadholder broke his alliance with France and joined with the English. The ministers of war and navy, Ségur and Castries, resigned. Brienne yielded once again. On July 5 he promised to call the Estates-General. On August 8 he suspended the Plenary

Court and set the date for assembly of the Estates-General
at May 1, 1789. On the twenty-fourth, the Treasury being
empty, he turned in his resignation. The king reluctantly
recalled Necker, whose first concern was to consummate the
retreat. Lamoignon was dismissed and on September 23 the
Parlement of Paris was reinstated.

The issue now seemed settled. The Estates-General were
now to meet. But who the beneficiaries were to be was soon
made clear by the Parlement, which ruled that the Estates
should be constituted, as in 1614, in three separate orders or
houses, each having the same number of deputies and possessing a single vote, so that the clergy and nobility would
retain the upper hand. The aristocracy had won its point.

The aristocracy had formed a common front against the
royal power. The intendants acted indecisively against such a
coalition of courts, estates and upper clergy. Bertrand de
Moleville, intendant of Brittany, excused himself from using
force against the Parlement of Rennes. Army officers declined
to obey orders. The aristocratic class developed an organization for political action, exchanging correspondence and
passing instructions from town to town. The Committee of
Thirty, which was soon to take over the leadership of the
Third Estate, seems to have originated as a center of parliamentary resistance. In Brittany the nobility of the sword
and of the robe, acting together, created committees in all
the important cities, to which they dispatched delegates to
stimulate action and give instructions. The aristocracy did not
hesitate to appeal to the bourgeoisie to gain its ends. Lawyers
lent their support, and shopkeepers who lived by service to
the parliamentary and noble families were aroused to make
demonstrations. In Béarn and Dauphiny, even the farmers
and sharecroppers were mobilized. In some cases the troops
were propagandized. None of these revolutionary precedents
was to be forgotten. The Parlements especially taught the lesson, for their reiterated remonstrances, their annulment of

compulsory registration, the attitude of the Parlement of Paris after the royal session of November 19, 1787, its declaration of fundamental laws, the interdictions laid by some courts on collection of taxes, were to find equivalents in the history of the Constituent Assembly; and indeed the Parlement of Paris went even farther than the Constituent Assembly in presuming to bring legal action against a minister, Calonne, who thus became the first *émigré*.

The question was now whether the Third Estate would let itself be shepherded by the aristocracy. That depended on the aims of the latter. These were clear enough to contemporaries, but it has since been maintained that the nobility and clergy were willing to admit fiscal equality, while imposing on the king a constitutional regime with a guarantee of essential liberties, and that the bourgeoisie was at fault in not ranging itself purely and simply behind their banner.

There is no doubt that the aristocracy, in its petitions of grievances in 1789, formally demanded the drafting of a constitution, the voting of taxes by the Estates-General and the turning over of administration to elected Provincial Estates. It showed itself equally solicitous of individual liberty and freedom of the press, if not freedom of conscience. In principle this program was formulated for the benefit of the whole nation, and its success would certainly not have been without advantage to the Third Estate. But it must be admitted without qualification that the Third Estate, had it been satisfied at this point, would have been obliged to accept a subordinate position in the state, because it was the intention of the nobility to control all estates, both general and provincial. "My uncle," said Mme. de La Tour du Pin, "wanted all France to be governed by estates, like Languedoc."

As for equality in taxation, it must first be noted that the privileged groups were never unanimous in accepting it. In its assembly of 1788 the upper clergy had once again claimed immunity from taxation for its property. It is true that the ecclesiastical petitions of 1789 sounded a different note, but this is because at that time the parish priests made themselves heard, and also because concessions seemed necessary after the Third Estate began to agitate. Even in 1789 the nobility of Upper Auvergne, Carcassonne and Rouen rejected fiscal equality; that of Dauphiny accepted it, but on condition that an indemnity be paid for noble lands hitherto tax-exempt. Other petitions of 1789, both of the clergy and of the nobility, made exceptions of the so-called personal obligations: quartering of troops, road service, militia. Others demanded a partial exemption. There should be special consideration for the parish priests, stated the clergy of Lower Limousin. Poor gentlemen should be spared, affirmed the nobility of Upper and Lower Marche. Upper Limousin wished complete immunity for the nobleman's residence plus "a few acres," and Lower Limousin for gentlemen who had less than 1,200 livres a year. These were impoverished areas. But in the district of Coutances we find immunity demanded for "an equitably determined portion of property," and in that of Caen a demand for "some exemption."

Even supposing unqualified acceptance of fiscal equality, the final word would not be said. Many petitions—more often those of the clergy than of the nobility—demanded that each of the two privileged orders allocate its own share of the taxes, or at least that their members be listed in special rolls, or that they should not have to pay directly to the parish collector but only to the general receiver, or that their tax should have a special name, for example "noble subvention." The aim is evident; even in fiscal matters distinctions were to remain, despite equality, between the aristocracy and the commoners. There was all the more reason for wishing to preserve the other noble prerogatives. The petitions of the nobility without exception called for the maintenance of the feudal rights and especially the honorific rights. The petitions showed the exclusivist tendencies mentioned above, demanding an end to the sale of offices and automatic creation of new nobles, a preferred status for the nobility at least in military commissions, free schools for their sons and noble chapters for their daughters. There can in fact be no doubt that the aristocracy had entered the struggle against absolutism in the name of the nation, but with the firm intention of governing the nation and especially of not being absorbed into it.

It is true that certain noblemen had less narrow views. These men, in the Estates-General, were to ally themselves with the Third, take the initiative in surrendering privileges on the night of August 4 and vote for the Declaration of the Rights of Man and the Citizen. It is not that they had abandoned the hope of keeping their leadership in the modern state, but rather that they were willing to count simply on the prestige of their names, the influence of their wealth and the claims of their own abilities. They hoped also to create an upper chamber where they would have a free hand. Had they had their way, France would have received a system analogous to that of England after the Revolution of 1688. The essential fact is that they consented to being legally no more than citizens of France. But they were only a minority; otherwise the Revolution would have taken place by common accord.

Should the Third Estate have contented itself, respectfully and submissively, with what the great majority of the aristocracy was willing to offer it? In any case it did not think so, and loudly demanded equality before the law. At this point, strictly speaking, the Revolution of 1789 began.

PART II ⊕ THE BOURGEOIS
REVOLUTION

CHAPTER 3   *The Bourgeoisie*

THE Old Regime threw indis-
criminately into the Third Estate all commoners from the
wealthiest bourgeois to the poorest beggar, or some 96 per cent
of the nation, according to Sieyès. The Third Estate was a
purely legal entity in which the only real elements were the
social ones—and of these the most important, the one
which led and mainly benefited from the Revolution, was
the bourgeoisie.

From the beginning the bourgeoisie had issued from the
peasantry by a continuous process. In 1766 Messance wrote
in *Traité de la population:* "No sooner is there a man too
many in the rural districts than he goes to town, becomes a
laborer, artisan, craftsman or merchant, and if he is busy,
economical and intelligent, and if he is fortunate, he is soon
rich." No barrier divided town and country in France as it
did in central and eastern Europe, where the peasant was forbidden to go into trade or industry, if, indeed, he was not
bound to the soil. Very much to the contrary, though the
bourgeoisie was mainly concentrated in cities, more and
more families in France in the eighteenth century lived "in
bourgeois fashion" in small country villages—lawyers, doctors, merchants, holders of invested income. The bourgeoisie
was intermixed with the rest of the population. That is why it
was able to assume the leadership of the Revolution. Yet it was
a minority, even if we add to it the skilled craftsmen of the

cities; for France, especially at that time, was essentially agricultural. And even this minority was not homogeneous within itself.

Levels of the Bourgeois Class

Finance and wholesale trade held the topmost place. The financiers had grown up in the service of the king. They included the bankers to the Court, the purveyors and contractors who supplied the army and navy with all kinds of transport and provisions, and above all the "farmers-general." These were wealthy men who formed companies to operate the "farm" or concession by which the government "farmed out" the indirect taxes, receiving an assured fixed sum, and leaving the farmers to make collections and retain the proceeds. For centuries the kings had treated the financial classes lightly, overwhelming them with favors when they needed them, then obliging them spasmodically to disgorge. Affairs were no longer run this way in the eighteenth century. Financiers were grand personages, allied by marriage with the aristocracy, cultivated men, sometimes learned, sometimes writers or patrons of the arts—for example Lavoisier, Helvétius, Dupin de Francueil, La Popelinière, Laborde. With them may be classified Treasury officials not yet raised to the nobility. In addition, toward the end of the Old Regime, Paris saw a great increase in the number of bankers. They were foreigners and Protestants for the most part, especially Swiss like Necker, or Clavière the future Girondist, or Panchaud the founder of the Bank of Discount, but among them were Dutchmen like Vandenyver and Englishmen like Boyd. For all of them the making of government loans was their main business, but on the eve of the Revolution the first stock companies were founded, the Paris water company by Périer, life and fire insurance companies by

Clavière. Speculation on the Stock Exchange developed; both Calonne and the financiers sought to manipulate the exchange through hired pamphleteers such as Mirabeau and Brissot. Loans to the king, to the clergy, to the provinces created a special class of bondholders, or *rentiers*, who lived almost exclusively in Paris, and who, being very sensitive to fluctuations in public credit, played an important role in the crisis of 1789.

For merchants the chief source of wealth continued to be sea-borne commerce, which occupied a great place even in trade between provinces of France, since wheeled vehicles could with difficulty transport heavy or unwieldy goods and the canal system was still embryonic. Colonial trade was considerable. From the "islands"—the French Antilles and particularly Santo Domingo—came sugar, cotton, indigo and tobacco. Quantities of these goods arrived from the eastern Mediterranean as well. Most exports likewise went by sea. The islands moreover had to be supplied with "ebony," as the black slaves procured in Africa were called.

According to Chaptal, exports in 1789 reached 438,000,000, imports 637,000,000, of which 250 represented goods from the colonies, so that the balance was favorable. The merchant was not yet specialized; he might be at the same time a shipbuilder, broker, transport agent, insurance underwriter, banker and manufacturer. The most powerful of these men were established in the ports, especially at Nantes, Bordeaux and Marseilles; but they were to be found also further inland at the great centers of distribution and industry, Rouen, Orleans, Lyons. They were to form, in time, the solid framework of the constitutional monarchist party, called "Feuillant," and later of the Girondists.

Industry remained socially and economically subordinate. It was in general an auxiliary to commerce. The merchant, at Lyons for example, gave orders to craftsmen who worked at home and received the raw material from him.

Concentrations of capital were in commercial form, and had received a strong impetus in the eighteenth century through the development of rural or cottage industry, to which the king granted complete freedom in 1762. In Flanders and Cambrésis, in Picardy, eastern Normandy and Champagne, in Brittany and Maine, in Languedoc, millions of peasants worked for city merchants. But the capitalists had also founded factories. At Reims, Sedan, Louviers, cloth workers were gathered in centralized establishments. Growth of this kind was not rapid, for, excepting the foundries at Anzin, no French enterprise yet used the steam engine. The factory system was necessary only in certain new industries that required expensive machinery: the cloth printing set up by Oberkampf at Jouy, found also in upper Alsace; the wallpapers produced at Paris by Réveillon in the Faubourg Saint-Antoine; the chemical products that made the fortune of Chaptal at Marseilles; the cotton thread spun by jennies recently brought in by Englishmen.

The merchant manufacturers, extremely protectionist as may well be imagined, were to exercise an obscure but powerful influence on the tariff policy of the Revolution and the Empire.

It would be wrong to exaggerate the importance of centralized or large-scale production. Most consumers were supplied locally by craftsmen who sold directly to the public. Some crafts like the Six Gilds of Paris were highly esteemed, and those who exercised them counted as notables, but there was wide variation both in wealth and in social standing. Legal status of craft production also varied, differing with different trades, different cities or even different neighborhoods in the same city. One craft might be "free," another organized in a gild or "corporation" endowed with a monopoly, from which in the eighteenth century hardly anyone benefited except the "masters," the heads of shops, who, however, were obliged, if enjoying this privilege, to observe standards of production watched over by the gildsmen. Suppressed by Turgot in 1776, restored after his fall, the gilds were increasingly criticized by the advocates of economic freedom. Their finances, moreover, had been burdened by the king's habit of creating new masterships, which the gild had to buy up in order to preserve its monopoly. Independent craftsmen were no more contented; they were menaced by the growing competition of the factories, and were obliged to hire themselves out to merchant employers who reduced them to the level of wage workers.

So the skilled workers and craftsmen were in general hostile to capitalism. From their ranks were to be recruited the *sans-culottes*.

The liberal professions also belonged to the bourgeoisie. They furnished a great majority of the revolutionary personnel. Lawyers of all kinds—judges, solicitors, notaries and barristers—were especially numerous, for there were many more courts than there are today, and manorial justice lived on in numberless rural parishes. Doctors were relatively rare, though some were famous, like Tronchin, Guillotin, Cabanis and Vicq d'Azyr. People in the villages and small towns contented themselves with an apothecary or "surgeon" as limited in social position as in professional knowledge. Laymen were prevented by the church monopoly from making great careers in teaching. Some laymen found places in the Collège de France, the Botanical Gardens and the faculties of law and medicine; most were only schoolmasters or private preceptors in a modest and dependent status. Printers and booksellers, men of letters and pamphleteers were of more importance, at least in Paris. Their world was a motley one, including lawyers without cases, like Desmoulins and Brissot, and unclassed nobles, like Mirabeau, who took to their pens to make a living. To them the Revolution was to open a career.

Bourgeois Attitudes

The bourgeoisie, in short, pre-
sented an extreme diversity of condition which was reflected
in their manner of life. The upper bourgeoisie of finance and
commerce lived in superb residences in the newer quarters of
Paris and the chief cities; only birth distinguished them from
the aristocracy. The life of most bourgeois was very different.
They were often not well-to-do: Cournot in his *Recollections*
tells how his grandfather, a notary, earned eight hundred
livres a year and yet brought up ten children. They were
thrifty, of frugal or even austere habits; the women knew
nothing of the luxury of the toilet. The family remained very
compact, the powers of the father very extensive. It is important to notice that these bourgeois were in close contact with
the common people. With a little savings, they would buy
land and watch carefully over their sharecroppers and hired
hands. The master craftsman would work side by side with
his laborers and journeymen, the latter called his "compan-
ions" in French. In city buildings the bourgeois would
occupy the ground floor and the floor above, the common
folk living further upstairs. This intimacy explains in part the
moral ascendancy of the bourgeoisie and the spread of the
revolutionary ideas by word of mouth.

For centuries the bourgeois, envious of the aristocracy,
had aimed only at thrusting himself into its ranks. More
than once he had succeeded, for a great many nobles
descended from ennobled bourgeois. This ambition was not
extinct. The Rolands put themselves to much trouble to get
themselves recognized as nobles; the Derobespierres cut
their name in two; Danton spelled his as d'Anton; Brissot,
son of an innkeeper of Chartres, blossomed forth as Brissot
de Ouarville, or still more fashionably, de Warville. Such
were the marks of gentility. Bourgeois of old stock were

frankly proud of their lineage, careful not to form an improper marriage. Officeholding and the professions established among them a hierarchy of which they were exceedingly jealous, and which engendered "cascades of disdain," as Cournot put it. Nothing was more pronounced than the ordering of ranks within this bourgeois society. The wife of a solicitor or notary was called "Mademoiselle." The wife of a councilor was "Madame" without dispute, and the wife of a barrister, or "graduate" as people said then, was usually saluted with the same title. Distinctions no less fine were placed between the doctors and the surgeons or apothecaries; the former had entered the bourgeoisie; the latter were knocking at the gates. Briefly, the bourgeoisie, looked down upon by the high born, copied them as best they could. It has therefore often been thought surprising that this class, whose spirit was so far from democracy, should have been so imprudent, in attacking the aristocracy, as to strike at the very principle of social hierarchy itself.

But the bourgeoisie had its reasons. The abolition of legal hierarchy and of privilege of birth seemed to it by no means incompatible with the maintenance of a hierarchy based on wealth, function or calling. Since at best only a small number of bourgeois could enjoy the advantage of becoming nobles, the rest of them wound up by execrating what they envied without hope. The exclusiveness of the nobility in the eighteenth century made the ascent even more arduous than before, especially when the nobles tried to reserve the most distinguished public employments for themselves. At the same time, with increasing wealth, the numbers and the ambitions of the bourgeois continued to mount. Sacrifices willingly made for the education of their children were meeting with disappointingly little reward, as the correspondence of Sieyès with his father testifies, and still better the examples of Brissot, Desmoulins and Vergniaud. The young Barnave wrote, "The road is blocked in every direction." Throughout the century government administrators had expressed alarm at the spread of education, and even in the Year III (1795) Boissy d'Anglas was to fear that education would result in forming "parasitic and ambitious minorities." With the doors shut, the idea arose of breaking them down. From the moment when the nobility laid claims to being a caste, restricting public office to men of birth, the only recourse was to suppress the privilege of birth and to "make way for merit." Pure vanity played its part, we may be sure; the most insignificant would-be noble nursed the wounds of his injured pride at the mere sight of the social distance above him. Among bourgeois of diverse kinds was forged a link that nothing could shatter—a common detestation of the aristocracy.

But it would do them an injustice to represent them as guided only by their own interests or narrowly personal resentments. The bourgeoisie of the West—first among them the middle class of England—had worked out a conception of life and society that was no doubt suited to its origins and its role, but which in its eyes was valid for all mankind. In the Middle Ages the Church, without reproving the search for well-being, emphasized preparation for death and the future life, the essential unimportance of material conditions of existence, the merit to be gained by renunciation and ascetic living. Here was a conception of life and society that may be called static, for scientific and technical progress, to say the least, was unavailing for the salvation of souls. The bourgeoisie put its emphasis on earthly happiness and on the dignity of man; it urged the necessity of increasing the former and elevating the latter, through the control of natural forces by science and the utilizing of them to augment the general wealth. The means, it was believed, consisted in granting entire freedom to investigation, invention and enterprise, for which the incentive was to be personal gain, or the charm of discovery, struggle and risk. The conception was dynamic, calling upon all men, without distinction of birth, to enter into a universal competition from which the progress of mankind was to follow without end. The ideas appeared in a confused way in the France of the Renaissance; subsequently Descartes inaugurated a new humanism by opening up a magnificent perspective, the domination of nature by science; finally, the writers of the eighteenth century, encouraged by English and American influences—here we must note Voltaire, the encyclopedists, the economists—set forth with spectacular success the principles of the new order, and the practical conclusions that it seemed fitting to deduce.

The works of these writers strengthened oral propaganda in the *salons* and *cafés* which multiplied in the eighteenth century, and in the societies of all kinds which were founded in great numbers—agricultural societies, philanthropic associations, provincial academies, teaching institutions like the Museum at Paris, reading rooms, Mesmerist societies where the magnetism put in vogue by Mesmer was experimented with and, finally and above all, Masonic lodges, brought over from England in 1715. The philosophy of the day inevitably entered into the conversations and colored the debates in all these organizations. It can be seen in the subjects for which academies offered competitive prizes. The topic set by the Academy of Dijon provoked Rousseau's famous discourse *On the Origin of Inequality Among Men*. The Masonic lodges in particular, though they included not only bourgeois but priests, nobles and even the brothers of Louis XVI as members, were favorable to philosophic infiltrations because they had the same ideal: civil equality, religious toleration, liberation of the human personality from all institutions which kept it immature.

By such different avenues the thought of eighteenth-century writers penetrated the bourgeoisie, giving it a full consciousness of historic mission. Historians for a long time exaggerated the importance of this moral and ideological preparation, even to the point of seeing in it the sole cause of the Revolution. Reality is mutilated if we overlook the play of practical interests in producing the revolutionary spirit. For the last half century students have applied themselves, and rightly so, to the task of showing how the revolutionary spirit originated in a social and economic movement. But we should commit no less an error in forgetting that there is no true revolutionary spirit without the idealism which alone inspires sacrifice. Undoubtedly the interest of the bourgeoisie, which was the first to profit from the new order, can easily be detected beneath the philosophy of the eighteenth century. But the bourgeoisie believed sincerely that it worked for the good of humanity. It was persuaded that it prepared the way for the advent of justice and right. Indeed the entire Third Estate believed the same. The men who rose on the great "days" of the Revolution, who fought at Valmy, Jemappes and Fleurus, would not have risked their lives had they been thinking only of themselves.

CHAPTER 4   *The First Victory*
              of the Bourgeoisie

To MAKE trouble for a min-
istry from which they expected no good, many bourgeois,
especially the lawyers, had taken sides with the Parlement of
Paris. Others remained neutral in that contest, such as
Roland and Rabaut-Saint-Etienne, the latter drawn to Paris
by the project for an edict favoring Protestants. In any case,
in the summer of 1788 there was no reason to anticipate that
the bourgeoisie would intervene, in the name of the whole
Third Estate, in the conflict between the royal power and the
aristocracy. But a wave of excitement passed over the bourgeoisie at the news that the Estates-General were to be convoked. For the first time since 1614 the king was authorizing
the bourgeoisie to speak. At first, no struggle was foreseen. It
was thought that the king, since he was calling upon his
subjects, meant to take account of their grievances. As for
the aristocracy, it had claimed to speak in the name of all
Frenchmen, and its spokesmen gladly called themselves
leaders of the "nation." The assembly at Vizille had left a
deep impression by conceding double representation to the
Third Estate, vote by head and fiscal equality. Agreement
seemed by no means impossible.

   But the outlook changed abruptly when the Parlement of
Paris on September 23 ruled that the Estates-General should

be constituted as in 1614. A clamor rose from one end of the kingdom to the other. Between night and morning the popularity of the Parlement vanished. "Never," according to the memoirs of Weber, "was a revolution in opinion so profound; never did enthusiasm turn so quickly to denunciation." The bourgeoisie stopped talking of despotism. Making an idol of Louis XVI, they turned their attack against the aristocracy. A social struggle, a "class war" as M. Sagnac has said, broke out openly. "The controversy has completely changed," observed Mallet du Pan in January 1789. "King, despotism and constitution are now minor questions. The war is between the Third Estate and the other two orders." Mme. Roland and Rabaut-Saint-Etienne now took passionately to public affairs. Brissot wrote, just back from a visit to the United States: "Scarcely six months had passed since I left France. I hardly knew my fellow countrymen on my return. They had advanced an enormous distance."

In aligning themselves against the privileged classes the bourgeoisie took the name hitherto claimed in common by all who opposed the royal power. They formed the "national" or "patriot" party. Those of the privileged groups who had unreservedly adopted the new ideas ranged themselves on the same side; they included great noblemen, the duc de La Rochefoucauld-Liancourt, the marquis de La Fayette, the marquis de Condorcet; and certain members of the Parlement, Adrien du Port, Hérault de Séchelles, Le Pelletier de Saint-Fargeau. These men, to take lead of the movement, joined with bankers like the Labordes, academicians like the lawyer Target and jurists and writers of note, such as Bergasse and Lacretelle, Servan and Volney. The party organized itself for propaganda. Like the Parlements and the Breton nobility before them, each man made use of his personal connections. Correspondents in the depths of the provinces did the same. Ties created by clubs and societies were certainly very useful. Since 1786 true political organizations had appeared in Paris—a Gallo-American Society, a Society of Friends of the Blacks, which demanded abolition of slavery, and political clubs in the strict sense, for example, the one at the Palais-Royal. These last had been forbidden by Breteuil in 1787, but Necker again tolerated them. The general staff of the new party met in certain drawing rooms, like that of Mme. de Tessé, soon to be Mounierís Egeria. Journalists harangued in the *cafés*—the café de Foy, the Caveau at the Palais-Royal, the Régence near by and the Procope on the Left Bank.

The question is whether a central intelligence directed this orchestra of protest. Such a role was soon attributed to Masonry, and the Revolution was explained as the result of a Masonic "conspiracy." No proof has ever been furnished. Many of the revolutionaries—not all—were Masons, and no doubt they found it easier to understand each other for that reason. But many aristocrats sat also in the lodges. The directing authorities of the several branches of Masonry, especially the Grand-Orient, could not have ordered their aristocratic members to lend aid to the Third Estate without provoking protests and schisms of which no cases are known.

A directing role can apparently be attributed only to the "Committee of Thirty," of which unfortunately we know very little. It met especially at the house of Adrien du Port, and its membership is said to have included the duc de La Rochefoucauld-Liancourt, La Fayette, Condorcet, the duc d'Aiguillon and certain ecclesiastics including the abbé Louis, the abbé Sieyès, who was a canon of Chartres, and Talleyrand, who was then bishop of Autun. Mirabeau also came to the meetings. This committee inspired pamphlets, circulated models for the petitions of grievances, supported candidacies and dispatched agents to the provinces, sending Volney, for example, to Rennes. Some of its members were wealthy, able to finance such activity. There is no reason for believing the Committee to have been in the service of the duc d'Orléans, although Sieyès and Mirabeau were certainly in contact with that personage. The duke had his own powerful resources—money, a veritable government of his own administering his vast appanage and a swarm of people dependent upon him in one way or another. He too had his agents draw up political instructions and model grievance lists, in which the hand of Sieyès can be detected. His own electoral campaign strengthened that of the bourgeoisie. But the influence of the Committee of Thirty and of the duke would be greatly exaggerated were we to imagine that everything done, in every town, was merely in execution of their orders. The state of communications allowed no such strict central control. If the movement prospered, it was because the local bourgeoisie showed its initiative; and experience was to show, during the early years of the Revolution, how jealously the provincial bourgeoisie insisted on their local autonomy.

The "Doubling of the Third"

The propaganda met with few obstructions. On July 5, 1788, in promising to call the Estates-General, the king had invited all his subjects to study the precedents for such an assembly, and to propose such changes as modern conditions might require. He had not intended thereby to grant freedom of the press, but on the pretext of responding to his appeal writers set forth their views freely, at least in pamphlets, into which they slipped such ideas as they pleased. The number of these pamphlets astonished contemporaries. The one by Sieyès, launched in January 1789, has remained justly celebrated for its emphatic formulas: "What is the Third Estate? Everything. What has it

been until now? Nothing. What does it ask? To be something." The trenchant tone of the first two of these pro-
nouncements, and the revolutionary hostility toward the
aristocracy which they reveal, have diverted attention from
the moderation of the Third, which nevertheless expressed
the character of the early stages of the patriot campaign.

The patriot party, in fact, by no means asked that the
Estates-General be elected without regard to the three
orders. On the contrary, seeming to fear the prestige of the
privileged persons and to think them capable of imposing
on commoners to the point of being elected to represent
them, the patriot party often demanded, even later on, that
each order be required to choose its representatives from
among its own members. The Third Estate, though it
already considered itself the "nation," was content to
demand the same number of deputies as the nobility and
clergy combined. This was called "doubling the Third." In its
favor was cited the example of the Estates of Languedoc, the
provincial assemblies and the assembly of Vizille. This
demand, it is true, was a very important one, for it implied
voting by head (not by order), which, indeed, the propagan-
dists often expressly stipulated also. Since the Third Estate,
under voting by head, could count on the liberal nobles and
most of the parish priests, it would obtain the majority, and
the aristocracy would no longer be able to force its conditions upon the king, or to keep the Third in a subordinate
position. But, in law, the double representation of the Third
Estate did not predetermine the method of voting. From the
consequent ambiguity the Third Estate could draw nothing
but an advantage, through weakening the resistance of one
part of its adversaries. The bourgeoisie from the first move
showed shrewd political sense.

As for executing the program, the scheme was to over-
whelm the government with a flood of petitions, for which
the municipalities, whether willing or not, were obliged to

take the responsibility during the autumn of 1788. At Dijon, for example, the matter was put through as follows: Some twenty "notables" met and decided to submit, to their respective gilds and corporate bodies, the questions of doubling the Third and of vote by head. The lawyers' association was the first to act favorably. It was followed more or less rapidly by others. By December 11 twenty of fifty such gilds had been won. The municipal authorities were then called upon to declare themselves. They consented to the doubling, but not the vote by head. Deputies from the gilds then invaded the hall. Under this pressure the city fathers yielded. The lawyers were charged with drafting a petition to the king in the name of the Third Estate of Dijon. In the other towns and larger villages of Burgundy events moved in substantially the same way, though sometimes the people concerned were more numerous. In some places peasants and workingmen streamed into the hall, and the whole Third Estate signed the petition.

By such means the bourgeoisie set the "nation" into motion. Its maneuver was denounced then, and has been denounced ever since. But the aristocracy, shortly before, had acted no differently. Every political movement naturally has its instigators and leaders. No one has ever dared to maintain that the Third Estate, invited to appear in the Estates-General, could have thought it natural to leave the aristocracy supreme in that assembly. Hence, what the leaders of the patriot party are blamed for is simply to have roused the nation to shake off its torpor and organize itself to defend its cause.

In addressing their petitions to the king, the bourgeoisie were really counting on Necker. This man from Geneva, son of a Prussian immigrant, had come to seek his fortune in Paris, and, having made it, had risen in society. His wife held a *salon* and gave dinners; his daughter, in 1786, married the

Swedish ambassador, the baron de Staël. His house was open to men of letters, who repaid their generous patron by giving him a reputation as an innovator and *philosophe*. During his first ministry, Necker got the Court on his back by some minor reforms, and his dismissal made him a popular idol. His writings on financial administration and his dispute with Calonne enhanced his reputation still further. He was thought capable of miracles.

He was an adroit technical man, and, as a banker and a Protestant, he could obtain, up to a certain point, the cooperation of foreign financial interests, not only in Paris but in Switzerland and Holland. He succeeded in keeping the state alive for a year in the worst of economic and political circumstances. He managed to get credits and he loaned his own money to the king; he made the Bank of Discount contribute; and above all he resorted to "anticipations," i.e., he gave creditors a lien on future income from taxation. What a windfall for high finance! Necker knew perfectly well that this was a temporary expedient. His only hope was to gain time, until the Estates-General could balance the finances by abolishing the tax exemptions. To leave the aristocracy the power to decide this matter would mean, at the least, abandoning the king to aristocratic mercies; Necker therefore inclined toward strengthening the Third Estate, without, however, committing himself to its cause.

Necker thought that all might be reconciled by a doubling of the Third and by granting the vote by head for financial questions only; thus tax exemptions would disappear, but the orders would come to blows over constitutional reforms, leaving the king in the position of arbiter. A statesman would have sensed the risk of uniting all sides against him, and would have seen what it was necessary to do: namely, to prevail on the king to state authoritatively the reforms he would accept, and then to take action to assure a favorable majority for this program. But Necker was exceptional in neither intelligence nor character. He had no comprehensive views of the work to be accomplished, and, if he had had, he was scarcely in a position to put them into effect—a point often overlooked by those who have condemned him. He knew the weakness of the king, the influence of the queen and the princes and the way in which the privileged interests had made an end to his own predecessors. His personal inclination, moreover, was above all things to remain in office, which he found flattering to his self-esteem. Like Calonne, he sought to act indirectly.

Necker convened the notables again, imagining, despite the first experience, that he could persuade them to pronounce in favor of "doubling." The assembly met on November 6, 1788. At Necker's first timid allusions, the prince de Condé vigorously protested. "Doubling" was rejected by five of the six sections into which the members divided for deliberation. On December 12 the princes of the blood sent the king a supplication which may be considered, in its clarity and its note of pathos, the best manifesto of the aristocracy: "The State is in peril . . . a revolution in the principles of government is preparing . . . soon the rights of property will be attacked, and inequality of wealth will be set up as a matter for reform; already the suppression of feudal rights has been proposed. Can Your Majesty bring yourself to sacrifice and humiliate your brave, ancient and respectable nobility? . . . Let the Third Estate stop its attacks on the rights of the first two orders . . . let it restrict itself to seeking a reduction of the taxes with which it may be overburdened. Then the first two orders, recognizing in the Third the citizens who are dear to them, may renounce, in the generosity of their feelings, the prerogatives which relate to pecuniary matters, and consent to bear public taxes in the most perfect equality."

At the same time, as was to be expected, some of the privileged were inclined to grant the Third Estate a certain satisfaction of its pride. On December 5, 1788, the "nationals" in
the Parlement of Paris prevailed on that body to declare, by
a formal order, that it had no intention of prejudging the
number of deputies in the Estates-General, and that the
number was not fixed by any law. In the Assembly of Notables the section presided over by the comte de Provence, by
a vote of thirteen to twelve, pronounced in favor of "doubling," on condition that each order in the Estates-General
should remain free to accept or reject the vote by head. In
private, some of the privileged expressed themselves definitely in favor of the Third Estate—for example, the comte
de Saint-Chamans and his sister Mme. de Meulan, whose
daughter later married Guizot. François Pateau, lord of
Maulette, wrote to the comte de Surgères, president of the
intermediate bureau of the provincial assembly of Île-de-
France: "Some think the non-privileged, who are the base
and pillar of the State, should be without sufficient representatives in an assembly which is to regulate their destiny.
That is really too insulting, and will not work. In any case,
the thing has been seen through. It will be best to be careful
of what is done. . . . But I perceive, my dear count, that I am
repeating to you what you know and think." Several of the
ministers, including Montmorin and Saint-Priest, sided
with Necker. The queen, vexed at the fall of her protégé
Brienne, seemed inclined to give a lesson to the aristocracy.
Necker judged that he could go ahead without the advice of
the notables, and, in fact, he had his way.

On December 27, 1788, an act called the *Result of the
Council* (an unprecedented term which seemed to leave the
king personally uninvolved) ruled that the Third Estate
should have as many deputies as the clergy and nobility
combined, without specifying whether voting in the Estates-
General should be by order or by head. It has generally been

concluded that the government committed a blunder by leaving this question open instead of settling it definitely before the meeting of the Estates. This opinion is not well-founded. Necker himself had pointed out that vote by order was the law, and that unanimous agreement of the three orders would be necessary to replace it with vote by head; having made this point clear, he was amazed at the storm over "doubling," which in itself made no difference. Judicially the meaning of the *Result of the Council* is thus incontestable: the principle of vote by order was upheld. But, politically, the document was none the less open to valid criticism. On the one hand, the text of the *Result* was silent on this point, at a time when it may have been indispensable to prevent ambiguity. On the other hand, Necker had maintained that the Estates could not be denied the right to adopt vote by head if they found it convenient. He had even added that this procedure might seem to them most convenient in matters of taxation. One can hardly fail to conclude that such was the desire of the government. Apparently, if Necker did not have this thought stated completely in the *Result*, it was because he realized that the king would not consent. It was no less evident that the Third Estate and the privileged classes would read opposite meanings in the text, and that consequently the Estates-General would, from the first meetings, be a prey to dissension.

Were any doubt left on this matter it was soon removed. The Third Estate exulted, affecting to see the vote by head already won. The aristocracy denied this interpretation, and protested no less violently against the "doubling" which made such an interpretation seem possible. The nobility of Lower Poitou came together spontaneously to protest. The Parlement of Besançon drew up remonstrances. On January 6, 1789, the Provincial Estates of Franche-Comté, assembling under the ancient forms, protested likewise. In Provence the nobility did the same, with the result that the Third Estate refused to sit in the Provincial Estates. In Brittany the class conflict degenerated into civil war. The Breton Estates met on December 25, 1788, but the Third refused to deliberate until the nobility and clergy consented to pay a fair share of certain exceptional provincial taxes, as had long been demanded by the Third. Bands of men recruited by the nobles, on January 26, 1789, came into conflict with the law students, led by the future Republican general, Moreau. The students won the battle and besieged their opponents in the hall of the Breton Estates. The young men of Nantes took arms on learning the news, and marched off to bring aid to the patriots at Rennes. The Breton nobles refused to elect deputies to the Estates-General, and were never represented in that body.

In the face of the aristocratic resistance, from November 1788 to February 1789, many bourgeois became more radical in their ideas. The Breton deputies, from the first meetings of the Estates-General, were to be resolutely opposed to conciliation. Rabaut-Saint-Etienne, in October, still favored an English system with two chambers, of which one should be made up of the two privileged orders; he defended honorific privileges as a barrier against democracy, which in his eyes was no better than anarchy. In December he wanted one chamber only, with vote by head. Sieyès especially, in his famous pamphlet, *What Is the Third Estate?* gave expression, with cold violence, to the hatred and scorn inspired in him by the aristocracy. They wished, he said, to exclude the Third Estate from honor and from office. Yet "who would dare to deny that the Third Estate has within itself all that is necessary to constitute a nation? . . . Take away the privileged orders, and the nation is not smaller, but greater. . . . What would the Third Estate be without the privileged orders? A whole by itself, and a prosperous whole. Nothing can go on without it, and everything would go on far better without the others. . . . This privileged class is assuredly foreign to the nation by its do-nothing uselessness." And the conclusion to be drawn was drawn clearly by Mirabeau, in the speech which he intended to make in the Estates of Provence, and which his exclusion therefrom, on February 3, 1789, reduced him to printing. Mirabeau eulogized Marius: "less great for having vanquished the Cimbrians than for having exterminated the order of nobility in Rome." Exterminate the nobility! Fearsome words! The *sans-culottes* in 1793, and Sieyès again in the Year VI, were to echo them.

The Elections of 1789

Meanwhile the government was preparing an electoral ordinance, which was published on January 29, 1789. It was not the only one, for various exceptions were granted, as was the custom of the Old Regime. Paris was made a special case, not ruled upon until April 23. In Dauphiny the Provincial Estates were authorized to name the deputies from the province, a favor demanded by the aristocracy everywhere else in vain. Plans for the elections remained imperfect in details. The map of the electoral districts, called bailiwicks, needed retouching; and administrative geography was so uncertain that some parishes remained in dispute between two or more bailiwicks.

The bailiwicks were territorial subdivisions whose origin went back to Philip Augustus. Their principal officers, in the early days, had combined all powers in themselves, but by 1789 they were merely honorific personages, called Great Bailiffs, and the bailiwicks were merely judicial districts. Over the centuries they had greatly increased in number, and had become incredibly unequal in size and population. For purposes of the election a distinction was drawn, somewhat at random, between "secondary" and "principal" bailiwicks. For the two privileged orders the distinction made no difference,

but for the Third Estate it meant that delegates to the bailiwick assembly, instead of electing deputies to the Estates-
General, sent some of their number to sit with delegates from
other bailiwicks, the resulting inter-bailiwick assembly then
electing the deputies to go to Versailles. Thus for the Third
Estate, where secondary bailiwicks existed, an additional step
was introduced between the original voter and the national
deputy.

Some opinions had been expressed in the Assembly of
Notables in favor of limiting the vote, even for privileged
persons, to those paying a certain sum in direct taxes. No
such requirement was adopted for the privileged orders. All
hereditary nobles were admitted to the bailiwick assembly
of their order, in person or by proxy, whether or not they
were in possession of a fief. But those with no fiefs received
no individual invitations; they complained that on this
point they were treated like commoners. As for newly made
nobles, with personal title only, they were thrown into the
Third Estate. All bishops and parish priests were likewise
admitted in person or by proxy, whereas canons and members of monastic orders could merely send representatives,
the latter only one for each house. Hence, in the bailiwick
assembly of the clergy, the parish priests were assured of an
overwhelming majority. This was a rude blow to the aristocracy, since, while the bishops were all nobles, the parish
priests were almost all commoners. The nobility, meeting in
person in their bailiwick assemblies, named their deputies
to the Estates-General directly. Among the clergy, the same
was true of bishops and parish clergy, while for other clergy
the election took place in two steps. Whether a bailiwick was
principal or secondary made no difference.

For the Third Estate the electoral system was far more
complex. Directly or indirectly, payment of some tax was
prerequisite to voting. In the towns the primary elections
went by gilds, persons belonging to no gild meeting in a

body of their own. Journeymen, in principle, were supposed to vote; but at Reims the drapers invaded the assembly, causing a riot, which had to be put down by force; and in fact the gild assemblies either included the master craftsmen only, or were dominated by them. In Paris it seemed impossible to organize the vote by gilds, and voting went by neighborhoods or districts; but only those paying a poll-tax of six livres qualified, with the result, it was said, that 50,000 heads of families were excluded, not to mention grown sons living with their parents. In the country, men twenty-five years old, and listed on the tax rolls, were admitted to the parish assembly. Grown sons were excluded, but all heads of family, or almost all, were thereby qualified. The rural suffrage was very liberal, if not universal. The peasants were favored in this respect because nobody was afraid of them. Each parish sent one delegate for every hundred hearths to its bailiwick assembly, in which, therefore, the rural population enjoyed a heavy majority.

But the mechanism of voting took away much of the democratic element in the system, and allowed the bourgeoisie to prevail over the peasants. For one thing, representatives of the Third Estate were in no case elected directly, but always in two, three or four steps. In Paris, they were elected by district delegates, hence in two steps. In other towns, delegates from the gilds elected a town delegation, which proceeded to the bailiwick assembly, where it then named, in concert with other town delegations and with delegates from the rural parishes, the representatives to sit in the Estates-General. The representatives, therefore, were chosen in two steps so far as country voters were concerned, and in three steps so far as town voters were concerned—or in three or four steps, respectively, in cases where secondary bailiwicks existed.

Moreover—and this is the main point—no one voted privately, as today, simply by presenting an electoral card, neither nobles nor ecclesiastics nor commoners. All voters, at each of the successive steps, formed themselves into an assembly. In assemblies electing deputies to the Estates-General each member came forward to cast a ballot when his name was called. In all lower assemblies voting was by word of mouth. Since in addition they had to draft a collective list of grievances the assemblies were not purely electoral, but deliberative as well. This is what allowed the most influential bourgeois, or those best informed on public affairs or most accustomed to speaking in public, namely the lawyers, to dominate throughout the debates. In the bailiwick assemblies the peasants, lacking education and unable to express themselves, let themselves be docilely led. The result was that the representation of the Third Estate was made up uniquely of bourgeois. That a few agriculturalists were elected is no real exception, for these men were not farmers in the strict sense, but farm managers allied to the bourgeoisie in their interests, if not indeed in their manner of life. The composition of the Third Estate in the Estates-General would have been very different, if, as some of the aristocrats had proposed and some of the grievance-lists requested, the government had created a separate order of the peasants, or had at least provided for the election of different deputies by the towns and by the country. Composed partly or in a majority of peasants, the Third Estate would have lost much in ability and authority, and probably in audacity, even granting that bourgeois and peasants would have agreed perfectly in their views, which is very uncertain.

The elections took place in February and March. Necker was urged to organize a "machine" which could submit a program of reforms to the electoral assemblies, together with candidates committed to support them. "You should have a settled plan of concessions and reforms which could consolidate the basis of legitimate authority, instead of undermining it." So an intendant of the navy, Malouet, himself a

candidate for the Third Estate for Lower Auvergne, wrote to
Necker. "This plan, through your influence, should become
the text of all the bailiwick petitions. You should not wait for
the Estates-General to plague you with requests and orders.
You should make haste to offer all that intelligent people can
desire within reasonable limits of authority on the one hand
and the rights of the nation on the other." He himself had
a project ready. But Necker dared not adopt such views. His
reasons remained the same. Before a plan of reforms could
be drawn up, the king would have to impose sacrifices on
the aristocracy without yielding to its demands. Necker was
convinced that at the first word the aristocracy would successfully intervene and force his dismissal. "Perhaps you
are right," he replied to Malouet. "You see the largest possible role for the Commons. But you take no account of
the resistance of the first two orders. To get the king to take
this line would alienate from him the nobility and the
clergy, who are still a great weight in the balance." His corre-
spondent answered: "It is not the resistance of the first two
orders that alarms me, but the exaggerated demands of the
Commons."

Did others step into the place which the government
declined to fill? The privileged classes had the means. They
had the chairmanship of each bailiwick assembly. At Saumur
the notary Rossignol obtained signatures to a protest because
the chairman had tried to influence the delegates. In many
parishes the peasants met under the chairmanship of the
manorial judge, and it is certain that in many cases they
dared not speak freely. But the bourgeoisie refused to be
intimidated. In any case the attempts of the privileged class
were confined to individual cases.

The patriot party was far more active. The Committee of
Thirty, as noted above, assumed a lead whose extent it is
impossible to determine. It is hardly doubtful that enterpris-
ing bourgeois everywhere took concerted action to steer the

town and bailiwick assemblies, with as many parish assemblies as possible in addition, by suggesting candidates and circulating models for the petitions of grievances. The models were either received from Paris, or, more often, drafted locally. Many lawyers lived in the villages, or often visited them for manorial pleadings, and they were very influential. Much aid was given by village priests who were at odds with manorial lords, whether through conflicts of interest, or rivalry for local influence, or injured pride or genuine devotion to the cause of their parishioners. Since 1789 there have been political parties with a much stronger organization than the patriots of that time, but none has ever met with so little resistance on the part of a government.

The nobles generally declined to elect members of the court nobility, liberals and (needless to say) nobles of recent origin. La Fayette was elected with great difficulty at Riom. In all bailiwicks the parish priests won a part of the seats for themselves, and in many of them they eliminated the bishop. The Third Estate preferred to elect men trained in the law, and in any case men from its own order, except that it did elect three priests and about a dozen noblemen as its representatives. Sieyès, rejected by the clergy of Montfort-l'Amaury, was one of these priests, and the dozen nobles included Mirabeau and a few noblemen by personal title.

The deputation of the nobles included some men of talent, but circumstances were against their making their weight felt, and most of them withdrew into a policy of abstention as soon as the Third Estate won its victory. The best known speaker of the noble opposition was Cazalès, deputy from Rivière-Verdun, an army officers, son of a councilor of the Parlement of Toulouse. Among the nobles, only the liberals played an important part: La Fayette above all, and after him Lally-Tollendal, Clermont-Tonnerre, the vicomte de Noailles, the duc d'Aiguillon and Mathieu de Montmorency. Du Port, a deputy from Paris, and Charles and Alexander de Lameth, from Artois and Péronne, were to figure in 1790 among the leaders of the patriot party. The duc de La Rochefoucauld became an influential and much heeded speaker on business affairs.

The clergy found an able defender in the abbé Montesquiou, and supplied the counterrevolution with a vehement and courageous spokesman in the abbé Maury. Among the bishops, again it was only the liberals that gained a notable position, especially Talleyrand, bishop of Autun, Boisgelin, archbishop of Aix, and Champion de Cicé, archbishop of Bordeaux, who became constitutional minister to Louis XVI. Few parish priests distinguished themselves. The best known of them was assuredly the abbé Grégoire, curate of Embermesnil and deputy from the bailiwick of Nancy.

The representatives of the Third Estate, who were soon to lead the Estates-General in its new form as the Constituent Assembly, were for the most part mature men in comfortable circumstances and enjoying honored positions—either in Paris, like the lawyer Target and the astronomer Bailly, both academicians, or Camus, a legal adviser to the clergy; or in the provinces, like the lawyers Mounier and Barnave in Dauphiny, Merlin de Douai in Flanders, Lanjuinais and Le Chapelier in Brittany and Thouret in Normandy. The youngest were almost all over thirty and enjoyed at least a local reputation, like Robespierre and Buzot. All were educated men, proficient in some specialized calling, hardworking and honest. Most were attached passionately to the cause of their class, which they did not distinguish from that of the nation. Many were enthusiasts for their mission. Those who like them the least cannot deny that they were a distinguished group, to which the greatness of their work, debatable enough in one way, still testifies beyond dispute. Yet it is also characteristic that, at least at first, the most prominent leaders were men from the privileged classes.

From this fact one may judge the prestige still possessed by the aristocracy, and what a place the aristocracy might have retained in the state had it been willing to compromise.

The marquis de La Fayette, made famous by the American war, enjoyed an incomparable prestige for about a year after the fall of the Bastille. As the "Hero of Two Worlds" he has remained the incarnation of the bourgeois revolution. His sincerity, disinterestedness and generosity surrounded him with a halo, but he was more a man of romantic illusions and somewhat juvenile vanity than of political skill or realistic sense. He was more a symbol than a leader.

The abbé Sieyès and the comte de Mirabeau also drew attention, for other reasons. Sieyès was the son of a moderately placed notary of Fréjus, who had pushed him into holy orders in the hope of making him the support of the family and especially of his two brothers. As a commoner, Sieyès could not rise to a bishopric; he had had a long wait before becoming even a canon of Chartres. His frustrations may have contributed to his violent animosity against the aristocracy. His pamphlets made him an oracle. In his eyes the Third Estate was the nation, and he, more than any other, seems to have led the Third in the early weeks. The nation alone, he insisted, possessed the power of sovereignty, and its representatives were therefore invested until the constitution was written with a dictatorial authority. Sieyès was the theorist of the "constitutive power" and the moving spirit of the juridical revolution. But being neither a speaker nor a man of action, he was never known except to the bourgeoisie. After the fall of the Bastille he soon lost the ear of the Assembly itself. The social aspects of the popular revolution frightened him. He came to the defense of manorial dues and ecclesiastical property. Fearful of democracy and wishing definitively to establish the rule of "notables," he ended up by organizing the Bonapartist *coup d'état* of 18 Brumaire, so that by a strange destiny he became gravedigger to the political liberty for which he had been godfather. A man of singular cast of mind, which he applied to making constitutional law into a science (an abstract one at that), and to building up systems of government tirelessly and in minute and complex detail, he wrote very little but preferred to have people come to consult him, acting through others when he acted at all. He was soon left in solitude without ceasing to be respected.

The comte de Mirabeau seemed destined for a greater role. A deserter from the nobility, a vigorous spokesman for the Third Estate on many memorable occasions, Mirabeau was marked out as a leader for the patriot party, much like La Fayette, and he had far more substance than his rival—a quick and penetrating mind, a fertile imagination, a sense for realities, knowledge of men, oratorical gifts all the more valuable because they shone especially in improvisation and unfortunately also a total absence of scruples in his choice of means. Although indolent and poorly informed, he had such a knack for choosing and holding collaborators, who wrote speeches and pamphlets for him, that he still passes today for an inhuman worker and a walking encyclopedia. With all his advantages, he never managed to overcome the distrust which was only too well justified by his adventurous past and venal habits. His turbulent disposition, derived from his ancestry, and which the deplorable example of his parents could do nothing to discipline, had thrown him into disorderly living from his youth. His extravagances had been a scandal, and he had several times been imprisoned on administrative orders. Without resources, he had lived by his pen in the service of both Calonne and Calonne's enemies, or had sold his name to add luster to publications which certain speculators, like Clavière, scattered about to prepare for their manipulations on the Stock Exchange. That Mirabeau was capable of offering himself to the Court in return for money, all who knew him were certain. Necker could have bought him at any time. For these reasons, while he rendered the Third Estate great services, he never succeeded in controlling it.

In summary, none of these men was able to dominate the scene to the point of personifying the Revolution of 1789, which remained the collective achievement of the Third Estate.

Electors of each of the three orders, before choosing their delegates, drew up a *cahier de doléances*, or "list" of their grievances and suggestions for reform. There were as many such lists as there were steps in the electoral system, each higher assembly collating and consolidating the lists of the assemblies below it. Only the lists composed in the bailiwick assemblies were taken to the Estates-General, but for our purposes the primary lists, especially those from rural parishes, are no less valuable. They allow us to see the influences exerted in the lower assemblies, and sometimes to determine that model lists were proposed to them for adoption, and what models were used. Critically examined, the primary lists show more fully than the bailiwick lists the wishes and state of mind of the population.

Study of these parish grievance-lists reveals that models were very numerous and usually of local origin. This in turn proves that the provincial bourgeoisie, as has been said, though inspired by publications from Paris, nevertheless retained its independence. But assemblies that considered a model did not necessarily forego the right to combine it with others, or to prune it down to suit their particular situation or to fill it out with grievances of their own. Moreover, many lists are entirely original. In the bailiwick of Nancy, for example, the use of eleven different models has been proved: 33 parishes adopted one model or another, 12 combined two or more, 32 either saw no models or declined to use them. In the bailiwick of Arques only a quarter of the lists were influenced by models. The models invariably contained political demands. The fact that the peasants adopted models does not necessarily mean that they took much interest in the political aims therein stated, or even understood their implications. On the other hand, it must not be forgotten that the peasants, in the presence of a manorial judge, were far from saying in every case what was most on their minds. In brief, the parish lists are not a faithful mirror, the bailiwick ones even less so, for the latter too often deleted items in the primary lists which the bourgeoisie did not agree with or was not interested in.

From comparison of the bailiwick lists of all three orders it is clear that all were unanimous against the absolute royal power. All wanted a constitution which would place the voting of taxes and new legislation in periodic Estates-General, turn over administration to elected Provincial Estates and guarantee individual liberty and freedom of the press. On freedom of conscience the grievance-lists are often reticent or silent, or even hostile in the case of those emanating from the clergy. All, to be sure, remained monarchist, not even denying the king's right to initiate and approve legislation, nor questioning the integrity of his executive power, notably his free choice of ministers and his right to make peace and war and to conclude treaties. If they often envisage a reform of the Church and rearrangement of its revenues, they question neither its privileged status in public worship, nor its moral influence, nor its honorary prerogatives. Many French bourgeois, though far from all, had become Voltaireans estranged from Christianity, preferring in most cases the "natural religion" preached by the Freemasons and which Rousseau had relieved of its dryness by his effusions of feeling. But even these bourgeois had not thereby become "laic," as we say now; and convinced that religion was at least necessary for the people, they had no thought of separating the Church from the State.

The three orders also agreed on a number of technical reforms. The petitions inexhaustibly criticize the wastefulness of the government and its agents, the abuses in public finance, the evils of indirect taxes, the way in which direct taxes were imposed arbitrarily for want of systematic assessment of property values. It is noteworthy also that despite a lively concern for provincial and municipal autonomy—so great that provinces regarded themselves as "nations" (Artois, for example, speaking of the "Artesian nation") joined to France only by the personal tie of the sovereign (the king being duke in Brittany, king in Navarre, Béarn, etc.)—the petitions none the less reveal, in almost every case, a distinct sense of national unity, and consequently demand unification of laws, weights and measures, and a pushing back of all tariff walls to the frontiers. In substance, on political and administrative reform, the nation was one.

But agreement of the orders turned to radical dissension when they looked to their respective positions in the state. The nobility, as we have seen, conceded fiscal equality at most; it wished its other privileges maintained and reinforced. The Third Estate wished complete civil equality; some of its petitions showed, at most, a willingness for the aristocracy to retain some honorific distinctions. The threat to aristocratic fortunes remained somewhat unorganized. Hunting rights and the keeping of game preserves were to be regulated severely. It would be well to suppress certain of the more odious manorial rights, notably those that were vestiges of serfdom. Often enough it was proposed to declare manorial dues subject to commutation in a lump sum. The tithe was attacked in principle more frequently than the manorial dues, but there was a readiness to tolerate it if it was converted to a money payment and if the proceeds were set aside for the parish clergy and the poor. The king was advised in a fair number of petitions to amortize the debt by seizing part of the monastic revenues or even by selling monastic property. As for the lands of the nobility, they were never in question; they constituted a form of property as uncontested and inviolable as that of the commoners. Moderate, however, as the demands of the Third Estate were, they were formally submitted, and it was over these issues that the conflict broke out. The Revolution of 1789 was above all the conquest of equal rights.

On the whole, the grievance-lists leave the impression that Malouet was right in advising Necker to outline an official plan of reforms. The overwhelming majority of the Third Estate and of the clergy could have been rallied to the king by promise of a regime resembling what the Charter of 1814 was to give—equality before the law, access for all Frenchmen to public employment, a reform of the tithe, authorization to buy out the manorial dues, a redistribution of church revenues granting a large part to the parish clergy, the poor and the schools and an assurance that the government, in concert with the Estates-General, would undertake the correction of abuses and improvement of its methods of administration. It was still not too late, but there was no longer a minute to lose.

But the Court remained inert. Even worse, it seems to have been roused by news from the provinces to a state of annoyance with the Third Estate and with Necker, regarding him as an accomplice. The Court forgot its grievances against the aristocracy, while the latter reciprocated by not pressing its demands. Court and aristocracy came together in common defense of the traditional social order.

CHAPTER 5   *The Estates-General*

THE Estates-General assem-
bled on May 4, 1789, their first act being to take part, with
the Court and the king, in a solemn procession through the
streets of Versailles to the Church of Saint-Louis, where they
heard a mass of the Holy Spirit and a sermon by the bishop
of Nancy, Monseigneur de la Fare. The choice of Versailles
was most imprudent. Far from imposing on the deputies,
the magnificence of the Court could only strengthen their
prejudices, while Paris was at the same time close enough to
encourage them to be firm. It was also to be expected that
every clash in the Estates would produce a dangerous echo
in the capital. These risks had indeed been foreseen, and the
convocation of the Assembly in the provinces had been considered; but the difficulty of housing so many people in a
small city, the repugnance of the Court to spending weeks in
inconvenience and boredom and the attachment of the king
to his habitual hunting grounds turned the decision against
the project. The government, in its political ineptitude, had
done nothing to amend the ancient etiquette of the occasion, leaving untouched certain observances that were
bound to indispose the deputies of the Third Estate by
emphasizing the inequality of orders too crudely. The
deputies of the Third on the opening day marched directly
behind the guard, at the head of the procession, modestly
clad in the historic black costume of the French bourgeois,

and followed by the nobility gilded and beplumed. Similarly the parish priests, in black habit, were grouped before the bishops and cardinals. When the deputies went to pay their respects at the château the king took pains to express special regard for "his" clergy and "his" nobility. Nor were similar embarrassments avoided at the opening session on May 5. The three orders installed themselves in a newly built hall in the Rue des Chantiers, behind the Hôtel des Menus Plaisirs, which ran along the Avenue de Paris. When the king had seated himself and put on his hat, the privileged orders put theirs on likewise. The Third, defying the custom, hastened to imitate them; but when Louis XVI saw what was happening he again bared his head, so that all hats had to be quickly removed.

After a colorless address by Barentin, the keeper of the seals, who was opposed to innovations, Necker rose to speak in an atmosphere of excited silence. Another disappointment followed. Soon overcome by fatigue, he had to hand his manuscript to an assistant, who read for a long time in a monotonous tone of voice. The speech contained no program, only advice—to the privileged, to renounce their pecuniary privileges at once; to the Third, to show proper "gratitude"; to all, to determine by common agreement the subjects on which they might then deliberate in common. The Third left the hall weary and disillusioned. Malouet did not fail to protest to Necker that the political bankruptcy of the government would lead to ruin. Necker, believing his position already weakened, thought himself more powerless than ever. Mirabeau offered his services, but Necker, holding him in contempt, as did everybody else, turned him away.

On May 6 the nobility and the clergy met in the halls allocated to them. The Third, the most numerous, was left in possession of the throne room. The public crowded in and, since no tribune or speaker's stand was built until later, mixed freely with the deputies and offered them advice. The public formed the habit, never to be lost, of greeting the deputies with applause or catcalls.

Three Orders or a Nation?

The privileged orders immediately set to work at the verification of credentials, with a view to organizing their respective houses. The Third found itself in a difficult position. If it imitated the others, it would acquiesce in the vote by order; if it openly opposed vote by order, it would go beyond the law. The latter course was not distasteful to the men from Brittany and Dauphiny, especially the former; but more politic members were apprehensive. The deputies were unknown to each other, and it was impossible to tell how far they were disposed to go. It was evident that some were alarmed by the ardor of the Bretons. Dilatory tactics seemed called for. Just as the Third had often demanded doubling without mention of vote by head, now it demanded that credentials of the three orders be verified in common, as if this would result in no precedent. The Third alleged the importance for each order to know that the other two were legally composed, and hence to verify the legal election of all members in a joint session. Now that the Estates were assembled, the Third had a means of pressure, in that nothing could be decided unless it rendered its opinion in due form. Hence the Third refrained from organizing itself or giving the slightest ground for pretext that it was organized. No minutes were kept, no rules adopted, no administrative office set up. Only a "dean" was appointed to direct the debates. After June 3 the dean was Bailly. Even the name "Third Estate" was replaced by "Commons."

There were serious inconveniences. The sessions on many occasions were no more than turbulent public meetings.

There was the danger of being accused of obstructing the regeneration of the state, a charge that might trouble many members. Malouet on this ground advised conciliation. The Third, he said, like any newly elected assembly should consider itself organized provisionally, and hence nothing prevented it from sending delegates to the other orders to open negotiations. He was told that individual attempts were all that were possible. On May 14 he went further. The Third, he suggested, might solemnly declare that it would respect the property, rights and prerogatives of the first two orders; it could then demand vote by head in fiscal matters with certainty of obtaining satisfaction. He was rudely and roundly overruled and was thereafter suspected. At the same time everyone realized that these maneuvers, if they were not to become dangerous, must not be protracted, and that some new strategy had to be found. It was the clergy that furnished it.

The nobility had not let itself be shaken by the attitude of the Third. On May 6 it voted 188 to 46 against conciliation; on May 11 it declared itself organized as a separate house. But in the clergy the majority had been only 134 to 114, and it was soon clear that a prolonging of the issue might reverse the proportion. Even several bishops, Champion de Cicé and Le Franc de Pompignan, archbishops respectively of Bordeaux and Vienne, and Lubersac, bishop of Chartres, were inclined to concessions. Hence the clergy refrained from declaring itself organized, and decided to propose that the three orders name committees to confer on the situation.

This meant new perplexities for the Third. Le Chapelier upheld the view that conferences were not only useless, since the Third was resolved to make no concessions, but even dangerous, since if it named members to a committee the legal argument might be advanced that it was an organized body and that verification in common could no longer be an issue. But a refusal might alienate the clergy. On the motion of Rabaut-Saint-Etienne the proposal was accepted by the Third Estate on May 18. The conferences, held from May 23 to 27, came to nothing, because the nobility and the Third showed themselves equally obstinate.

From then on the tactics of the Third were to adjure the clergy, "in the name of the God of peace," as Mirabeau said, to come and join with it. On May 27 a delegation sent to the clergy, led by Target, was warmly received. A little later, on June 6, when the clergy, noting the food shortages, declared it urgent to deliberate on ways of relieving the people, the only answer was that a joint meeting of the orders was the more necessary for that reason. But in the interim the bishops, sensing the parish priests slipping away from them, had appealed to the king to intervene. On May 28 Louis XVI proposed a resumption of conferences in the presence of the ministers. On June 4 the ministry formulated a basis of agreement: each order should verify credentials of its own members; those that were contested should be reviewed in common by committeemen from the three orders, who would refer them to their respective houses; if no agreement was reached, the king would decide. For a third time the Third was embarrassed. Not daring to refuse arbitration by the sovereign, it postponed decision until the end of the conferences. At this decisive movement the nobility relieved it of having to pronounce. For on the same day, June 5, the nobles, by a vote of 158 to 76, ruled that the committees and the king might arbitrate only in cases of members of "total delegations" (those few bailiwick delegations which had been elected, like the one from Dauphiny, by the three orders combined) and that nobles elected by nobles were subject only to their peers. The conference on the next day admitted its defeat, holding only one more session, on June 9, to approve its minutes. This was the signal for revolutionary action.

A month had passed. Agitation was growing in Versailles and Paris. The feverish excitement of the public spread during the meetings to the deputies, who also used the time to advantage to become acquainted and establish relations with each other. The Bretons had created a "Chamber of the Province of Brittany." Meeting at the Café Amaury and soon called the Breton Club, this organization served as a center for representatives of the Third Estate. At the beginning of June Sieyès declared the moment come for "cutting the cable." On June 10 he proposed a summons to the privileged orders to come and join with the Third; in case of refusal, a roll call of all deputies regardless of order should be held anyway and those not appearing should be considered defaulted. The Third, in other words, should erect itself into a national representative body by its own will and without the king's consent. Target and Treilhard, with Sieyès' approval, obtained a change of wording from "summons" to "invitation," and the motion thus amended received 246 votes. But Regnaud of Saint-Jean d'Angély had also proposed presenting an address to the king with a statement of reasons, which Sieyès accepted; and 246 votes were cast for the motion accompanied by the address. The cautious and the hesitant desired in this way to diminish the unprecedented character of the motion, and even to suggest that such a motion required the king's approval. Fifty-one deputies voted for referral to committees or for rejection. It was vital for the initiative of the Third to have unanimity behind it. This was obtained, or nearly so, in an evening session, through joint adoption of the motion and the address. The combined roll call began on June 12 and went on until June 14. Three parish priests joined the Third on the thirteenth, six on the fourteenth, three more on the fifteenth. No noblemen appeared. La Fayette did not dare to break the mandate which bound him, and which forbade the vote by head.

The Third Estate could not act in the name of the Estates-General, which in any case would have perpetuated memories of division into orders. Another name was needed to express the unity rather than the diversity of the nation. The Third groped for several days before hitting upon one. On June 15 Sieyès proposed "assembly of the recognized and accredited representatives of the French nation," a formula that was somewhat equivocal in implying that the said assembly was incomplete. Mounier was more explicit, affirming that the assembly was in fact incomplete and suggesting that it call itself "the representatives of the greater part of the French nation acting in the absence of the lesser part." Guarded though these designations were, the very principle was disputed. It is probable that the opposition, by its explanations, contributed to a radical solution. Malouet fought against the position taken by Sieyès and Mounier because it implied suppression of the orders. Mirabeau, regarding the national sovereignty as belonging to king and assembly together, perceiving that the assembly without fully realizing it tended to appropriate complete sovereignty to itself and wishing to arrest the process in its early stages, suggested the title of "representatives of the people." A stormy debate ensued. He was asked whether he translated "people" as *populus* or *plebs*. If the latter, the assembly would represent only the common people, those neither nobles nor priests, and not the whole nation. This was in fact what Mirabeau meant, and it was another reason for viewing him with distrust. The majority, thus enlightened, found Sieyès' title insufficiently explicit. It seems in any case that Sieyès had the decisive proposal in reserve, and that Legrand, deputy from Berry, who presented it, was only his mouthpiece. However that be, it was Legrand who on June 16 asked the Third Estate to take the name of "National Assembly." This was carried on June 17 by 491 votes against 89. Almost a sixth of the representatives of the Third Estate thus disavowed the juridical revolution. The Assembly immediately made its first use of its newly assumed powers by authorizing provisionally, on motion of

Le Chapelier, the collection of all existing taxes. The implication was that the Assembly might prohibit collection if its
will were resisted.

The Tennis Court and After

Most of the clergy felt no
alarm at the audacity of the Third Estate. In fact, a majority,
including several bishops, voted on June 19 to unite with the
commoners. But since ten members had expressed reservations, the presiding officer, Cardinal La Rochefoucauld,
declared the motion lost, hastily adjourned the session and
rushed off to beg the king's intervention. The king had
already, on the fifteenth, received similar pleas from the
nobles, who, abdicating in favor of the royal power, as Lally-
Tollendal pointed out, and realizing somewhat late in the
day that their own social preeminence was in danger of col-
lapsing without the king's protection, had invited his
Majesty to bring the Third Estate back to its duty.

Louis XVI had just lost his eldest son, the Dauphin, who
died on June 4, and had retired to Marly. On the nineteenth
he decided to hold a "royal session" of the Estates on June
22, and he assembled the Council of State. On the need of
annulling the action of the Third and of authoritatively settling the question of verification of credentials and vote by
head, the Council agreed in substance but not in form. It
was admitted also that the time had come to draw up a program of reform, in which fiscal equality should be included.
But Necker thought this no longer sufficient, and declared
that bankruptcy was certain unless the Third was concili-
ated. He wished therefore to add accessibility of all Frenchmen to public office and an authorization allowing
the Estates-General to vote by head in determining their
future organization. This divided the Council. Montmorin,

Saint-Priest and La Luzerne supported Necker. Barentin, Villedeuil and Ségur objected. The last named, the minister of war, especially protested against any measure by which the king's hands should be tied in the appointment of army officers, and the king, much disturbed by this possibility, blamed Necker for having even thought of it. Finally, apparently after intervention by the queen, the decision was postponed until the twenty-first, and the royal session therefore deferred to the twenty-third. On Sunday the twenty-first the Council, reinforced by several persons, including the king's brothers, rejected the most important of Necker's innovations. On the next day it approved the definitive text of the decisions to be signified to the Estates-General by the king.

The postponement had given the Third Estate time to prepare its resistance. On June 20 it found the hall of the Menus Plaisirs closed and in the hands of workmen. The deputies found a haven in a neighboring indoor tennis court, which still exists. The crowd was great and the deputies very excited. Almost all, not excepting those who had been in opposition on June 17, were united by personal danger in a common resolution to stand firm. The most ardent, led by Sieyès, wished to move to Paris, where the assembly would be under popular protection. Mounier averted this revolutionary step by suggesting, as a substitute, an oath to remain assembled until a constitution was framed. The resolution was carried by acclamation:

> Whereas the National Assembly has been called upon to draft a constitution for the kingdom, effect the regeneration of public order and maintain the true principles of the monarchy, and whereas nothing can prevent the continuation of its deliberations in whatever place it may be obliged to establish itself since wherever its members are gathered there the National Assembly is in being;
>
> Be it resolved that all members of this Assembly shall at once take a solemn oath never to separate but to meet in any

place that circumstances may require, until the constitution of the kingdom shall be laid and established on secure foundations; and that after the swearing of the oath each and every member shall confirm this indefeasible resolution by signing with his own hand.

Bailly took the oath first, and 577 members signed at once, of whom 557 were deputies in their own right (not alternates) and five were originally from the clergy. Mounier's intervention had kept the conflict at a peaceful and juridical level, so that the Third avoided even the appearance of being the first to resort to force; but it had another advantage too, for it bound all members of the Third Estate solidly together. Only one, named Martin Dauch, representing the bailiwick of Castlenaudary, refused the oath. He explained that he could not engage himself by oath to carry out decisions which the king would not have sanctioned. Bailly replied that the intent of the Assembly was perfectly clear—constitution and laws would be submitted to the king for approval. But the answer was beside the point; what was at issue was the existence of the Assembly, and the Oath of the Tennis Court announced a determination to defend it even against the king. Not everyone gave his adherence gaily or lightheartedly. Mirabeau is supposed to have said: "I sign because otherwise you would mark me out for public hatred . . . but I tell you that we are signing a conspiracy." To prudence, also, may be attributed some of the absences recorded on that solemn day—55 deputies and alternates and 5 priests did not sign until the twenty-second. At least two deputies of the Third imitated Martin Dauch without having his courage, for they gave no indication of their opposition and simply abstained from signing. The general solidity of the Third Estate was only thereby accentuated.

On the twenty-second the Assembly found a more suitable meeting place in the Church of Saint-Louis, and most of the clergy came in a body and joined it. The nobles of

Dauphiny and a dissident group of nobles from Guyenne followed their example. The government's project was already thwarted.

At the royal session on the twenty-third, in the presence of an exultant nobility, with the Third Estate and parish priests sober and dejected, and with Necker absenting himself as a sign of his disapproval, Louis XVI announced that Barentin would make known his will. His speech declared the acts of the Third Estate null and void, but at the same time canceled the binding mandates, and hence those which forbade deputies of the privileged orders to accept the vote by head. Each of the three orders was confirmed in the right to verify credentials of its own members, but if a deputy protested his exclusion his case was to be judged by three orders combined and voting by head; if this decision was in turn rejected by a two-thirds majority of one of the orders, the king would have power to arbitrate. The king likewise authorized joint deliberation and vote by head in affairs of general interest, but from such affairs he expressly excluded "the ancient and constitutional rights of the three orders, the form and constitution of future Estates-General, feudal and manorial property, and honorific privileges and useful rights of the first two orders," and he stipulated that matters concerning religion or ecclesiastical organization must receive the specific approval of the clergy.

After the reading of the royal address the king himself spoke, announcing that the reforms acceptable to him would be laid before the Estates. "Never," he declared, "has a king done so much for any nation."

His program granted the Estates the right to consent to taxes and loans, and to determine the allocation of funds to the various public services, including the upkeep of the Court. The king promised to sanction equality of taxation as soon as the privileged orders had voted for it; the personal obligations were excepted, but might be replaced by an ordinary tax.

Individual liberty and freedom of the press were guaranteed. Administrative powers were granted to Provincial Estates to be elected by order, but with double representation for the Third and vote by head. The Estates-General would be expected to consider reforms in the administration of the crown domain, the salt monopoly, excise taxes, militia and courts of justice; they would be free also to suppress internal tariffs. Finally, compulsory road work and other such services, together with the vestiges of serfdom, were to be abolished.

For the third time the king spoke in person: "If you abandon me in this great enterprise I will work alone for the welfare of my peoples. . . . I will consider myself alone their true representative. . . . None of your plans or proceedings can become law without my express approval. . . . I command you to separate at once, and to proceed tomorrow morning each to the hall of his own order to renew your deliberations." The threat was clear: the Estates would be dissolved if they did not submit.

The program of June 23 is of the utmost interest because it shows clearly what was at stake, not only in the following weeks but in the whole Revolution. The king was willing to become a constitutional monarch, and so the purely political problem at least in principle was solved. Practical reforms were merely a question of time. But except for abolition of fiscal privileges, advantageous to the monarchy as well as to the Third Estate, the monarchy now threw all its influence toward preserving the traditional social forms, including the preeminence of the aristocracy.

Whether this program, laid out six months earlier, would have won the adherence of the Third Estate is very doubtful. In any case, it was now too late. Nothing but exasperation was produced by "the repulsive panoply of a *lit de justice*," as Ferrières called it, by the king's imperious tone and by his parting threats. Those who had favored conciliation now made common cause with the majority. "After the royal session," wrote Malouet, "we had no course but the one we took in the Tennis Court."

The nobility withdrew from the royal session as directed, but the Third, as agreed beforehand, remained in place, as did a few of the clergy. When the marquis de Dreux-Brézé, grand master of ceremonies, reminded them of the king's orders, Bailly responded: "The nation when assembled cannot be given orders." Mirabeau, from where he stood, cried out to the courtier the words that remained traditionally symbolic of the whole session: "We will not leave except by force of the bayonet."[8] Sieyès summed up, in his lapidary style: "You are today what you were yesterday." This amounted to saying that the Assembly, like the Parlements of former days, held the king's orders to be void. The Assembly confirmed its earlier acts and declared its members inviolable.

At the château the nobility received the king and queen with enthusiasm. Orders were given to clear the Third from the hall, but when the guards reached the doors they met some liberal nobles who persuaded them to go back. The crowd grew, a rumor spreading that Necker was to be dismissed. The king renounced for the moment the idea of using force: "Oh, well, the devil with it—let them stay." Necker received a tremendous ovation. It seemed prudent to allow unification of the orders. The nobles objected, and no less than a command from the king and a letter from the comte d'Artois were needed to make them yield. On June 27 the nobility seated itself in the National Assembly.

Hence was effected the bourgeois revolution, or what may be called a juridical revolution, realized without recourse to

---

[8] The Assembly having no stenographers, Mirabeau's words were not recorded at the time and cannot be reconstituted exactly. The phrase quoted above is the one concluding the text which Mirabeau printed in his *Lettres à ses commettants*. (Author's note)

violence, by methods taken over from the Parlements by men trained in the law. On July 7 the Assembly appointed a committee on the constitution, whose first report was presented by Mounier on July 9. Henceforward, and for history, the Assembly was the "National Constituent Assembly." On July 11 La Fayette submitted his proposal for a "Declaration of the Rights of Man and the Citizen."

It does not appear that the Third was disposed, at this time, to carry the consequences of its victory to an extreme. Its conception of its own authority was closer to Mirabeau than to Sieyès. Though the former, on June 23, had indeed spoken of the king as the "mandatory" of the nation, he maintained that sovereignty was undivided between the monarch and the Assembly. The Assembly had not brought into question either the hereditary monarchy or the need of having the constitution ratified by the king. In its eyes Louis XVI remained invested with a power of his own, given by history, and it was for the nation to negotiate a pact with him, as one equal with another. The modern constitutional conception, by which the constitution not merely regulates public powers but creates them integrally, was not yet clearly worked out. There was still no question of that dictatorship of constituent power of which Sieyès spoke. It was not yet denied that the king should freely approve or reject constitutional articles, as well as ordinary laws, or that he should keep the totality of executive functions.

Moreover, the three orders, though united in one Assembly, had not disappeared from the social structure of the nation. It had not even occurred to the Third to force the election of a new Assembly, so that nobles and priests retained their seats though representing an infinitesimal minority of Frenchmen. Of feudal rights not a word had been said. It cannot then be claimed that the Third contemplated a class rule.

The clergy, now that the commons had won unification and vote by head, were inclined to urge a conciliatory program. The clergy enjoyed great respect; on July 3 the Archbishop of Vienne was elected president of the Assembly. The minority of the Third which had shown its conservative tendencies on June 17 was certainly inclined in the same direction. It was the same with the liberal nobles, whose prestige was still intact and who seemed destined for a leading place in the government as well as in the Assembly, so great was the timidity still unconsciously felt by even the best known commoners in the presence of high-ranking aristocrats. If the rest of the nobility, accepting the accomplished fact, would collaborate in good faith with these various elements in the Assembly, a moderate majority might form itself which, along with the king, could establish a stable government and bring about the reforms by methods of compromise.

But this opportunity, which was very real, of keeping the Revolution a peaceable one and of restoring national harmony, neither the king nor the aristocracy for a moment dreamed of seizing. At the very moment of resigning themselves to unification of the orders, they decided to resort to force to restore the obedience of the Third Estate.

The majority of the nobility at once adopted a significant attitude. Many abstained from sitting; others attended only for form's sake and refused to take part in the discussions or the voting. They still alleged that their mandates forbade them to vote by head: The Assembly on July 8 annulled the binding mandates; the king then authorized the noble deputies to return to their bailiwicks to ask fresh powers from their constituents. Those commoners who had been skeptical of their adversaries' good faith grew increasingly suspicious from day to day, and the moderate majority could not be formed.

Meanwhile the king was concentrating troops in the neighborhood of Paris and Versailles. The first orders had been given as early as June 26. A pretext was readily found in the growing popular agitation, the multiplying troubles due to the food shortage and the indiscipline of the French Guards regiment, which provoked a riot in Paris at the end of the month. When the Assembly, disturbed, requested an explanation on July 8, after a violent diatribe of Mirabeau against military dictatorship, Louis XVI replied that he was obliged to keep order and that if the Assembly wished he would gladly transfer it to Soissons. He had called about 18,000 troops, who were to arrive from July 5 to 20. The food shortage and the poverty of the Treasury greatly hindered the troop movement and made it necessary to disperse the arriving units. Command had been given to Marshal de Broglie, who was represented in Paris by the baron de Besenval. It seems that Broglie, judging no action to be imminent, remained unprepared. Lacking initiative, he left Besenval without orders during the decisive days.

The Court certainly intended to dissolve the Estates. In the circumstances it could count on the support of the Parliaments and resign itself to bankruptcy. But it had no settled plan, and before forming one it had to get rid of Necker and assemble a ministry prepared to fight. Measures were discussed with the king on July 9; it was decided to call in the baron de Breteuil, who arrived the next day. Wisdom would have dictated setting up a secret government, to emerge in the open as soon as the troops then on the road had arrived. It was a fearful game to play; for while one can easily understand that a king by divine right would revolt at the thought of yielding once and for all to his people, in whom he could see nothing but rebels, and while one can realize, knowing its sentiments, that the aristocracy would regard surrender without a struggle as a mortal indignity, still the enterprise was in danger of degenerating into civil war, and if it failed the bloodshed would redound against the aristocracy and the king. Nevertheless, on July 11, at a council to which Necker was not called, it was decided to install the new ministry publicly and immediately. The Paris electors were urging the Assembly to authorize the formation of a bourgeois or civic guard, and indiscipline in the army was rapidly spreading; these were perhaps the motives in the Court's decision to wait no longer. Necker was dismissed and started for Switzerland; Montmorin, Saint-Priest and Ségur were dismissed with him; La Luzerne resigned. Breteuil and his aides took their place. But no action followed.

The Assembly expected force to be used. Some deputies, not daring to return to their quarters, spent the nights in the session hall. It was thought that at least a certain number would be arrested. The elder Thibaudeau, very much worried, was flippantly reassured by M. de la Châtre: "You won't hang—you'll only have to go back to Poitiers." The bourgeoisie put a good face on the matter, and all accounts testify to their firmness. But they could hardly have any illusions: they were at the mercy of bayonets. No speeches could save them. At this point the force of the people intervened, beneath whose blows the Old Regime went down beyond recall.

PART III ✦ THE POPULAR REVOLUTION

CHAPTER 6   *The Mobilization of the Masses*

ALL France had watched events with passionate interest. In Paris the newspapers talked little of the Estates-General until the end of June, but the curious traveled every day to Versailles, bringing back news to be discussed in the *cafés* and at the Palais-Royal, which was then much frequented, the garden and luxury exhibits in the arcades drawing great throngs. Not the least attentive were the holders of government bonds, who were fearful of bankruptcy and were irritated to the last degree by the dismissal of Necker.

In the provinces, since the newspapers remained silent, there would have been no source of news except travelers and private letters, had not steps been taken at the time of the elections to form committees which became agencies of information. In many bailiwicks the electors of the Third Estate, and in some those of the nobility also, had designated a few of their number to correspond with their deputies, i.e., to watch them. In other cases the deputies at Versailles kept officials at home informed. Generally their letters were publicly read. People would stream in from all directions when the mail coach arrived; at Rennes the hall where they met had to be especially propped up. Copies were made of messages from the deputies; at Rennes, Nantes and Angers they were printed.

These communications made some of the authorities suspicious, and the national deputies have since been accused, though without proof, of inciting to violence. The truth is that they feared violence, their thought being well expressed by Duquesnoy, deputy from Bar-le-duc, when he wrote that "one must work for the good of the people, but the people must do nothing for it themselves." Still the deputies naturally remembered the campaign of 1788, and set great importance on evidences of public opinion. They constantly urged their constituents to undo the maneuvers of the aristocracy by sending in testimonials supporting the National Assembly. A great many addresses from constituencies thus approved the vote of June 17, protested against the royal session and expressed satisfaction at the unification of the orders. In this way, it must be agreed, the deputies helped to stir up opinion.

It can hardly be doubted that, for other reasons, many prominent people in the cities were quite willing to go further. Municipal authority, where it was not in the hands of officials who had purchased their offices and were often newly made nobles, was practically confined to a small oligarchy connected with the various law courts, if indeed not almost identical with them. At Paris, for example, the provost of the merchants and the four *échevins* or "aldermen" were elected by a body which included the outgoing provost and *échevins*, twenty-four city councilors who had purchased their offices, sixteen *quartiniers* who were a species of police magistrates appointed by the Hôtel de Ville and thirty-two "notables" chosen by these *quartiniers*.

The bourgeoisie were bitterly jealous of these monopolists of local office, and would gladly have forced an opening for themselves into the city administrations. At Paris the 407 delegates of the several quarters of the city, who had elected the deputies to the Estates-General and were hence called electors, had thereafter kept up contact with one another; on

June 25, 1789, they met in the auditorium of the Museum in the Rue Dauphine, from which they moved to the Hôtel de Ville and set themselves up as an unofficial municipal government. In some towns local uprisings led to a municipal revolution before the fall of the Bastille. At Rouen and at Lyons the old corporations, under pressure, took in some of the notables and electors. The bourgeoisie thus won a political weapon for satisfying their ambitions, for when local power passed into their hands it passed into the service of the National Assembly.

It was equally advantageous for the bourgeoisie to create an armed force of its own. In Paris the maintenance of order was then entrusted to the "watch" under a lieutenant of police, who was an agent of the Crown, and likewise to the regiment of French Guards. Towns in the provinces had a civic guard, which however existed only on paper; in case of trouble they had to resort to the garrison, or ask for troops from the military commander of the province. From the spring of 1789, with disturbances multiplying, the civic guards had in some places been reorganized, but they remained under the legal authorities. What the bourgeoisie desired was a national militia electing its own officers and capable if necessary of independent action. In Paris the electors proposed creating one to the National Assembly, but that body dared not give its approval. The Paris electors argued, sincerely, that the lesser people must be kept in a dutiful frame of mind; but their aim was really twofold, to deprive the king of a pretext for calling troops to preserve order, and, if he called them, to resist.

Finally, it is certain that some bourgeois encouraged indiscipline in the army. They had little difficulty in doing so, for nobles monopolized the higher ranks, subordinate officers had almost no chance of promotion and the soldiers, who had to buy their own subsistence from their pay, suffered from the prevailing high prices. The French Guards in Paris, dispersed in small stations, constantly mingling with the townspeople and in some cases intermarrying with them, were at heart with the Third Estate. People took them to the Palais-Royal and to the *cafés* to buy them drinks, and we know that the marquis de Valady and a brother of André Chénier, former officers of this regiment, helped along the propaganda by distributing money.

The Working Class

When the decision of the Court to use force became clear, we may be sure that at least part of the upper bourgeoisie helped to organize resistance. Bankers like Laborde and wealthy merchants like Boscary, who boasted of it later, advanced funds to pay insurrectionists for their lost days' wages and to equip them with arms and ammunition. All categories of society are represented among those "conquerors of the Bastille" whom it has been possible to identify. Yet when the list is read over it becomes clear that the overwhelming majority of actual combatants were tradespeople from the Faubourg Saint-Antoine and the Marais Quarter. The strength of insurrectionary movements, throughout the Revolution, lay in the lesser bourgeoisie of handicraft workers and shopkeepers. Heads of workshops, not their illiterate journeymen, retail shopkeepers, not the mass of their illiterate customers, were the ones who circulated news and initiated demonstrations. They were the permanent personnel around which insurrections formed. Journeymen and workingmen gathered behind them, not as a separate class, but as associates in the small-scale industry of the time.

The wage-earning class was indeed already large. In Paris, for example, in a population estimated at 500,000 or 600,000, the wage workers may have numbered 75,000, or some

250,000 to 300,000 counting their families. In some lines of work they were concentrated—a shop making cloth, hats or wallpaper would employ from two to three hundred. They lived also, by preference, concentrated in certain neighborhoods. The western part of the city was then the domain of the wealthy. Between the public markets and the Hôtel de Ville, and from the Seine to the boulevards and beyond, lived more than 20,000 workingmen; on the Left Bank, from the Palais Mazarin to the Panthéon, another 6,000 at least. Moreover, workmen in certain lines, mainly the building trades, were strongly organized in journey-men's unions which had survived all attempts at repression and which conducted strikes more often than is thought. Yet when all is said, only a small minority of wage workers were yet assembled in factories, residentially concentrated or brought together in labor organizations. The famous revolutionary areas of the city, Saint-Antoine with its woodworkers, Saint-Marceau with its tanners, had an abundance of small shops in which master craftsmen and their journeymen employees fraternized on the great insurrectionary "days." On the whole the wage workers had no clear consciousness of class. If they had had, it is very doubtful whether the Revolution of 1789 would have been possible. The workers would perhaps have been willing to make common cause with the rest of the Third Estate against the aristocracy, but probably the bourgeoisie, as happened later in Germany, would have shunned the support of such formidable allies.

Master craftsmen and shopkeepers on the one hand, journeyman workers on the other, had their grievances against the Old Regime and detested the aristocracy, but they could not expect to win the same immediate advantages as the "notables" from a victory of the Third Estate. Important especially in their eyes was an alleviation of the tax burden, mainly by abolition of indirect taxes and of the local imposts from which the municipalities drew most of their revenues, to the great advantage of the well to do. On the craft gilds their views were far from unanimous. Politically, they tended obscurely toward democracy, but no one yet dreamed of promising it to them. It is in thinking of this group that one best realizes how the calling of the Estates-General assumed in the eyes of the people an almost mythical character. An event so strange raised a hope both radiant and nebulous, a hope for a national regeneration, a new era in which men would be more happy. It is in this aspect that the Revolution, at its beginning, can be compared to many religious movements in their early stages, in which poor men joyously see a return to the earthly paradise. This fire nourished the revolutionary idealism. But at the same time it ignited a whole complex of alarming passions.

Boundless hope was offset by a conviction that the nobles would stubbornly defend their privileges, a conviction which the bourgeoisie shared with craft workers and peasants, and which arose at least in part from a realistic sense that in their place each would do the same. The opposition to doubling, then to vote by head, rooted this conviction more deeply. It was thought that the king of course was benevolent, but that he was surrounded by aristocrats who bent him to their will, and who by many menacing phrases conveyed the impression that they would stop at nothing to crush the Third Estate. As early as May 15, according to one of Montmorin's informants, the people were convinced that the Estates-General would be dissolved by force; by June 27 they expected, he said, to see "the nobles appear on horseback." Périsse-Duluc, deputy for Lyons, declared that on June 23 there had been talk of dispersing, imprisoning and even executing the national deputies. At the end of June and beginning of July it was currently believed that the comte d'Artois, if he failed to have his way, would leave the country and ask for aid from foreign sovereigns. What could be more natural? Was not Louis XVI the brother-in-law both of the Emperor and of the King of Naples, and in addition the cousin of Charles IV of Spain? Were not his two brothers sons-in-law of the King of Sardinia? Périsse-Duluc recalled having foreseen, before the opening of the Estates-General, that the French aristocracy might follow the example of the counterrevolutionaries in Holland, who had called in the Prussians to win a victory over their own countrymen. Collusion of the aristocracy with foreign interests, which was to weigh so heavily on the whole history of the Revolution, was regarded as a fact from the beginning, and in July 1789 there was already fear of an invasion. The entire Third Estate believed in an "aristocratic conspiracy."

Anxiety often degenerated into panic after the Court launched its offensive. Yet there was nothing cowardly even in the "Great Fear" itself. Apprehension and terror produced a violent defensive and military reaction. In June, at Versailles, tumultuous crowds tried to intimidate the nobility and the Court. Preventive action was not long in following, with a train of suspicions, denunciations, house searches and arrests. These angry moves could not fail, after the victory, to arouse a will to punish the enemies of the "nation" and of the common well-being, which in turn led to summary executions and all the excesses of revenge.

Would the mass of the people have been less stirred by such hopes and terrors if a grave economic crisis had not been making their lives almost unbearable? Discussion of this question will never end. The fact is, in any case, that in most cities the motive force in the riots of 1789 was usually material want, and the first result a reduction of the price of bread. The revolts aided the Revolution in helping to dislocate the administration of the Old Regime, to the advantage of the bourgeoisie; but such was certainly not their purpose. On the other hand, certain details of the economic crisis strengthened and oddly elaborated the idea of an aristocratic conspiracy. It is therefore beyond dispute that the economic distress should be included among the immediate causes of the Revolution.

The Economic Crisis

As always in the old France, food shortage was due to a succession of mediocre or clearly inadequate crops. The French of that time ate a great deal of bread. Peasants and workingmen required no less than two or three pounds a day. The average daily consumption was later estimated by the Convention at a pound and a half, whereas the ration during the war of 1914 was only two-fifths of a pound. Except in the larger cities and in areas producing much wheat, the bread was generally of rye or buckwheat, or of a variable mixture of wheat, rye and barley. Despite backward methods of cultivation, France in the good years managed to be self-sufficient on the eve of the Revolution. The South never grew enough grain for its needs, but brought it in from Brittany and the North by sea, or from Burgundy by internal waterways. At the same time there was a general anxiety to have the granaries well-stocked. It was hard to get from one year to the next without a reserve, for except in the South, where the grain was threshed immediately with the help of mules, asses or oxen, the threshing was usually done with flails and was a long and laborious process which the farmers preferred to postpone until the winter, after the fall plowing was over. Meanwhile they had to have "old grains" to live on. Of these there was never thought to be enough, for without them famine was certain if the crop failed. It was not easy to move grain from one province to another, because transport by water was often impossible for want of canals, and by wheeled vehicles was slow and expensive. Supply by sea was irregular and relatively meager, the coastal craft weighing 200 or 300 tons at most, and often less than 100; nor could one ever be sure that foreign governments would not prohibit export at the most critical moment. Hence every region wished to keep its local grain supply and live on its own. Difficulty in communications did not allow much exportation in any case; the total export of grain from France seems never to have passed two per cent of the crop. Yet people eyed every outgoing shipment with misgivings, even if bound for another province of France. They feared not only famine but also rising prices, and the apprehension of consumers was shared by the authorities in their concern for public order, especially by the municipal authorities, which were the most vulnerable to disturbances.

Hence the grain trade was carefully regulated. Peasants were not allowed to sell grain outright, either at home or in transit. They were required to bring it to the town market and there display it before the eyes of the inhabitants, who had the right to buy it first, the bakers coming next, and the merchants last. The authorities intervened, when necessary, to apportion the available supply and even to set the price. In any case they kept a record of grain trading as the basis for the price of bread, which was controlled. The system sacrificed the farmer to the city dweller. The market occupied a place in daily life that we can scarcely realize today. Only the poorest households bought bread from day to day from the baker. People purchased grain for at least a week in advance, had it ground themselves and baked either at home or at the common or so-called "lord's" oven. Bread was generally bought from the baker only in the large towns, and not universally even there. The custom was most common in Paris.

The economists had demanded liberation of the grain trade from all controls, wishing to see prices as high as possible, so that the area under cultivation would be extended and methods of cultivation improved. In 1763 and again in 1774 free trade between parts of the country, by land or sea, had been permitted and sales outside the markets had been authorized. But the experiment had been soon dropped each time. Brienne had renewed it in 1787, and had even authorized export. A significant amount of exportation soon followed, whose effects have been somewhat unreasonably questioned, since even if the amount exported could not have been very large it still contributed to a lowering of reserve supplies, and with coastal traffic moving what was left from north to south, all provinces were stripped on the eve of the harvest of 1788. This harvest was a wretched one; prices rose beginning in August 1788 and without stopping until July 1789. One of Necker's first acts was to order purchases from abroad, grant subsidies for imports and restore exclusive sale in the markets. In April 1789 he even authorized the intendants to supply the markets by requisition. It must be added that in the wine country the crisis was preceded by another of opposite nature. For several years the grape harvest had been abnormally abundant, driving the price of wine very low. The high price of bread was felt all the more painfully by the wine growers, of whom there were a great many.

Poor crops and unprofitable sales had the same effect: they reduced the purchasing power of the masses. The high price of grain was especially disastrous in that even many of the peasants did not themselves grow enough to live on, particularly when the harvest was bad. The agricultural crisis provoked a crisis in industry. There were of course other causes. Contemporaries attributed a great influence to the Treaty of 1786, which granted the English a tariff reduction on certain manufactures, notably cottons and hats, in return for reductions on French wines and brandies. Since British industry was equipped with machines far superior to the French, its competition was blamed for the marked decline in French textiles on the eve of the Revolution. This decline did in fact date from 1786, but the truth is that the treaty in question did not go into effect until the middle of 1788, so that at most it aggravated the evil. The war which in 1787 brought Turkey to blows with Russia and Austria, and the unsettled conditions which resulted in Poland after withdrawal of Russian troops, likewise contributed to industrial depression in France by reducing exports to eastern Europe and the Levant. All international trade was suffering anyway, because the harvest of 1788 was bad everywhere in western Europe. So unemployment worked its ravages at the very moment when the cost of living was going up. Workmen could obtain no increase in wages. In the best of times wage rises were hard to get; it has been calculated that between 1726–1741 and 1785–1789 prices rose 65 per cent while wages went up only 22 per cent. In 1789 a Paris workman earned on the average some 30 to 40 sous a day. For him to live, it was estimated that bread should cost no more than 2 sous a pound. In the first half of July the price was twice this figure. In the provinces it was much higher, reaching 8 sous or more, because the government, fearing disturbances in Paris, had no hesitation in selling there, well below the current price, the grain which it imported from abroad. Bread had never been so dear since the death of Louis XIV. How can one fail to suspect a connection between this ordeal and the fever of insurrection that gripped the population at the time?

Popular Beliefs

The small people never resigned themselves to explaining scarcity and high prices simply by the weather. They knew that tithe owners and manorial lords who collected dues in kind had considerable stores of grain, which they withheld from sale while waiting calmly for higher prices. Even more bitterly they blamed the dealers in grain—the small merchants who went from one market to another, the millers and bakers to whom trade in grain was

forbidden but who engaged in it fraudulently. All were suspected of withholding, or hoarding, to precipitate or encourage a price increase. There was the same suspicion of
purchases made by the government and local authorities,
who were thought to make a profit either for their budgets or
for their own pockets. Louis XV, for having entrusted a business concern with the task of creating grain reserves for
Paris, was accused of lining his own treasury at the expense
of the peoples' food; there were few who disbelieved in this
"famine plot." Necker was likewise attacked for having an
understanding with the millers who ground the imported
grains, and who, so it was rumored, dishonestly re-exported
it in the form of flour. Freedom of the grain trade looked like
a blank check given to those who grew wealthy on the hard-
ships of the poor; and it is clear that, if the reasoning of the
economists was correct, the resulting progress nevertheless
benefited landowners and business interests, while the ordinary people, at least momentarily, bore the burden. The
economists judged that misfortune was the will of Provi-
dence, and frankly declared that social progress could come
only if the poor were willing to make sacrifices. The people
thought, and sometimes said, that they ought to be able to
live by their work, and that the price of bread should be proportionate to their wages; if the government gave a free hand
to business and property, in the name of the general interest,
then it should also take measures to assure the right of everyone to a living, by taking from the rich the wherewithal to
subsidize bakers or sell grain at a loss. But the method considered obviously the simplest by the small people was to
return to the old regulation, apply it with rigor and not recoil
from a system of requisition and price control.

It is not surprising that want and high prices were frequent causes of rioting. Sometimes the attack fell on those
thought to possess stores of grain or be trading in it; their
establishments were pillaged or they themselves were put

"to the lantern," i.e., hanged by the cord from which a street lamp usually swung. Sometimes it turned upon persons whose imprudent language, more or less accurately reported, had aroused public indignation. On April 28, 1789, a terrifying riot, put down by musket fire and executions, devastated the shops of Henriot, a saltpeter dealer, and Réveillon, a wallpaper manufacturer who was supposed to have said that workmen could live on fifteen sous a day. More often the scene of disorder was the market place; mobs pillaged the grain belonging to the peasants, or demanded action by the authorities. Often, too, people stopped the convoys which constantly circulated in all directions, by land and water, from farm to market, from one market to another, from town to mill and from mill to town, parading the desperately needed grains and flours before the eyes of the hungry. Soldiers and mounted police wore themselves out running from place to place; they too were pinched by the high prices, and were not without sympathy for the troublemakers. Lastly, the administrative and social authorities were assailed. A municipality was in as much danger as a tithe collector or manorial lord of falling victim to a mob. After the spring of 1789 there was hardly a town which had not seen one or more "incidents" or rebellions, and these were doubly frequent in July, because the trouble was at its worst on the eve of the new harvest.

The crisis shook the existing order no less violently in another way, by uprooting part of the population. Mendicity was an incurable evil because of constant unemployment, at least in the country, and because windows, the old and the disabled were left to shift for themselves, or almost so. Begging was not a disgrace; fathers having children to provide for sent them out "to find their bread." Beggars and unemployed left their own parishes, became vagabonds and descended upon the towns. Their numbers grew beyond belief in times of crisis. It was asserted in the Constituent

Assembly in 1790, after a survey, that 2,739,000 family heads, or some 10,000,000 of the French people out of 23,000,000, were in need of relief, and that 3,000,000 of these were to be considered paupers, i.e., beggars. The riots which desolated the towns were attributed by municipal authorities to outsiders, a much overworked theory, since at Paris, for example, the record of arrests shows that the great majority of the accused were unemployed residents of the city. Yet there is no doubt that vagrants added to the insecurity. In rural districts the situation was worse; homeless persons banded together and resorted to threats and actual violence. They were regarded as "brigands," and their ranks did in fact include troops of malefactors, salt smugglers and others who lived by contraband operations. The "fear of brigands" spread from country to town. Well before July 1789 local panics broke out. In May, at Montpellier, the brigands were expected to arrive by sea. In June, at Beaucaire, it was rumored that they were coming to loot the fair. On July 8, at Bourg, word spread that they had crossed the frontier from Savoy, an impoverished country whose wretched emigrants were well known. These alarms gave another incentive for demanding, and often obtaining, the formation of a local militia.

Between the "fear of brigands" and the fear of the aristocracy a connection was rapidly and generally formed. It was maintained from an early date that the aristocracy favored the hoarding of food, that it held back its grain in order to crush the Third Estate and that for the same reason it was not displeased to see the harvest pillaged or the crops cut down before they were ripe. Those who feared that the aristocrats were resorting to arms naturally expected them to recruit followers among vagrants and vagabonds, just as the kings' recruiting officers enrolled their men among the lowest class. Jails, prisons and almshouses were alike suspected as eventual sources of such levies. And since the nobles were expected to call on foreign troops, it was thought natural that they would also draw on "brigands" from neighboring countries. It was said in Paris, early in July, that 60,000 were on the way. The "aristocratic conspiracy," thanks to the economic crisis, seemed a monstrous machination not merely to prevent the Third Estate from liberating itself but to punish it by pillage and massacre. Feeling rose to the utmost pitch, and the dismissal of Necker was a torch applied to a powder keg.

CHAPTER 7   *The Paris Revolution*
                             of July 14

Alarms and Precautions

IT WAS on Sunday morning, July 12, that Paris heard of the dismissal of Necker. The day was fair, and a crowd assembled at the Palais-Royal in the afternoon. Amazement and consternation soon turned into indignation and fury. Orators gathered audiences by improvised speeches which they filled with imprecations. Only one speaker is known to us by name: Camille Desmoulins, who at about half past three raised the call to arms, brandishing a pistol. Soon demonstrators swarmed in the streets. The main body left the Palais-Royal at four o'clock, going off to close the theaters, which then opened at five or five-thirty. Busts of Necker and the duc d'Orléans, seized at Curtius' waxworks, were paraded on the boulevard. Returning to the Palais-Royal, the crowd started for the Champs-Elysées.

A unit of cavalry now intervened. But it met armed resistance from some of the French Guards, who appeared at the same time, taking sides with the people. The Royal German regiment, commanded by the prince de Lambesc, at about eight o'clock tried to drive the demonstrators from the Place Louis XV, now the Place de la Concorde. The crowd flowed back toward the Tuileries, and from a position on the terrace proceeded to stone the cavalrymen, who nevertheless continued to charge, knocking over and injuring several persons. No doubt there were other skirmishes of which we know nothing. Marat later boasted of having led a crowd against some soldiers at the Pont-Royal. Danton also is reported to have roused the quarter then called the Théâtre-Français, though the players had left it in 1771. It was the neighborhood of the present Odéon; here Danton lived, and here his statue was subsequently erected. Other lawyers and auxiliaries of the legal profession flung themselves, like Danton, into the movement.

Besenval, left without orders, concentrated his forces in the Champ-de-Mars. The deserted city fell prey to tumult and disorder. The poorer classes, remembering their own hatreds, rushed to the "barriers" and burned them. These were tollgates in the wall built around the city in 1786 by the tax concession. On the next day a mob pillaged Saint-Lazare, which was thought to be a storage place for grain. The police having disappeared, security of person and property was in peril. Apprehension descended upon Paris.

The worst had not yet come. What did the Court propose to do? No one guessed that it did not yet know, which was nevertheless the fact. On July 13 communications with Versailles were cut, since the Sèvres and Saint-Cloud bridges had been guarded by soldiers. At Versailles the Assembly seemed done for, and the Parisians were making no attempt to come to its rescue. If the events of July 14 saved it, they did so on the rebound, for it was their own fate that the Parisians were worrying about, and with reason. The king's troops seemed to have the city surrounded. On the north they might occupy the hill of Montmartre and set up batteries there. On the west they could join Besenval and his Swiss. On the south they could threaten the Left Bank. On the east was the Bastille, where the governor, de Launay, had moved cannon into the embrasures, bringing the whole Saint-Antoine area into his field of fire. Attacked and bombarded from all sides, the capital would be taken by assault and turned over to pillage. On July 17 the bookseller Hardy, of the Rue Saint-Jacques, noted in his journal that 30,000 troops supported by a great number of brigands had been ready for battle. Panic was continuous. During the night of July 13–14 it was announced at the Hôtel de Ville that 30,000 troops had entered the Faubourg Saint-Antoine, later that the Royal German was at the Throne Gate, still later that the enemy had penetrated the La Chapelle Gate. These rumors are known to us by the minutes of the Paris electors; there must have been many others. These days in Paris were simply the first act of the Great Fear.

But they produced a singularly prompt and effective military—and defensive—reaction. The tocsin rang on the thirteenth. The people, not content with guarding the city gates and carefully watching all entrance and egress, began to build barricades and arm themselves as best they could, soon emptying the shops of the armorers. The bourgeoisie took over leadership of the movement and tried to organize it, both to restore order and to make resistance more effective. As early as July 10 it had been proposed at the meeting of the electors to have a new city assembly elected. At that time the proposal had still seemed revolutionary. But on the twelfth it was adopted without discussion. Pending an election, power was entrusted to a permanent committee, which included the old provost of the merchants, Flesselles, his four *échevins* and a few councilors, but also a majority of the electors. Henceforth, through this body, the electors took charge of affairs, appropriated the public funds and gave orders to administrative officials. The bourgeoisie, thus gaining control in the capital, decided on the thirteenth that each quarter and district should furnish 800 men for a bourgeois or national guard. Soldiers from the French Guards offered their services, patrols began to circulate and houses were kept lighted at night.

It was the intention of the committee for the militia to be made up of known and reliable men, and to reserve for these men such arms and ammunition as it could procure. But the crowd thronged about the Hôtel de Ville, and, on the plea of self-defense, demanded guns. Flesselles temporized as best he could, but he had to send to the Arsenal and give out what few firearms he thus obtained. What was really going on was a general arming, for which the available resources were ridiculously insufficient. Hence the crowd streamed to the Invalides, where on the morning of the fourteenth it collected 32,000 muskets. Some looked in vain in the Carthusian abbey, behind the Luxembourg, for weapons rumored to be stored there. Searchers likewise found nothing at the Arsenal on the thirteenth but did learn that the Bastille was amply provided. This bit of information precipitated the decisive affair.

The Fall of the Bastille

Counterrevolutionary legend represents the people of Paris foolishly attacking the Bastille to deliver prisoners who were not there (practically speaking, since there were in fact only seven), and adds ironically that for many years the honors of the Bastille had not been reserved for the common people, which is entirely true.[9] Yet it is hardly doubtful that the famous state prison stood in the eyes of the populace as a symbol of despotism, and if the

---

[9] Confined in the Bastille on July 14, 1789, were two mental cases, an abnormal young man kept in custody by his family, which paid his expenses, and four men undergoing prosecution for forgery in the criminal courts. The Bastille at this time had become a place of discreet confinement for persons of note or influence.

vulgar made the mistake imputed to them they would have acted understandably enough, since what went on within its walls was quite unknown. Nevertheless, when the Faubourg Saint-Antoine milled about the Bastille, on the morning on July 14, their intention was not to attack it but to call on the governor to distribute the arms and ammunition in his possession, and incidentally to demand that he withdraw from the embrasures the cannon which menaced the city. With walls a hundred feet high and a moat seventy-five feet wide and filled with water, the Bastille was safe from any sudden onslaught. The garrison consisted only in eighty superannuated soldiers, reinforced by thirty Swiss under command of a lieutenant Louis de Flue. The old soldiers were on poor terms with the foreigners, and were persuaded with difficulty to fire on the people. The governor, the marquis de Launay, irresolute and incapable, had neglected to supply himself with provisions. These weaknesses were unknown outside. The idea of attacking the Bastille arose in consequence of events which could not have been foreseen.

The permanent committee, warned about eight in the morning of the popular tumult, sent three delegates to reassure de Launay and request him to withdraw his cannon. The delegates did not arrive until ten; the governor received them warmly and invited them to lunch. All sat down to the table. The crowd outside, which was now immense, wondering what had become of the delegates and supposing them to be prisoners, became increasingly excited, and its more fiery spirits now began to talk of calling on the fortress to surrender or else of attacking it. The electors of the adjoining district, informed of the growing feeling, charged one of their number, the barrister Thuriot, to bear a summons of surrender to de Launay. Thuriot observed that the cannon had been removed from the embrasures, and that the old soldiers seemed disposed to yield, but that the governor's staff persuaded him to do nothing. At this time the crowd had penetrated only the outer court, which was easily entered from the Rue Saint-Antoine, and which was separated by a wall from the inner, or Governor's Court, where the real gate of the fortress, with a long drawbridge, was located. The wall between the courts also contained a gate, with a small drawbridge. This gate de Launay had left undefended, simply raising the bridge. A half hour after Thuriot came out of the fortress, two men climbed the wall and forced the small drawbridge down. The crowd swarmed into the inner court, and de Launay, becoming excited, ordered his men to fire. Several of the attackers fell; the others recoiled in disorder, crying "treachery" and persuaded that they had been let in only to be shot down the more easily. Those who were armed began to fire on the defenders. The fighting continued, very unequally, for of the assailants at least 98 were killed and 73 wounded, whereas only one of the old soldiers was hit. Two new delegations from the committee, the second bearing a white flag, tried in vain to intervene, but were not spared by the garrison, and therein lay a new source of annoyance.

Still no decision was in sight when two detachments of the French Guards left the Hôtel de Ville with a certain number of bourgeois of the militia, led by Hulin, a former noncommissioned officer, and penetrated the two courts of the Bastille, bringing five cannon. They were joined by a lieutenant of the queen's regiment, named Elie. Under fire they placed a battery of three pieces in position before the main gate of the fortress. This operation was decisive. De Launay offered to capitulate, threatening to blow the place up unless terms were given. Elie accepted, but the crowd protested: "Down with the second drawbridge! No terms!" Despite the objections of Louis de Flue, de Launay, at his wit's end, had the second drawbridge lowered.

The crowd poured into the fortress. Leaders managed to save most of the garrison, but three officers of the staff and three old soldiers were massacred. All that could be done for de Launay was to get him, with great effort, as far as the Hôtel de Ville; there a band of men broke up his escort and put him to death. Shortly thereafter Flesselles was killed by a pistol shot. The two heads were cut off and paraded about the city on the ends of pikes.

Besenval, in the Champ-de-Mars, had not budged all day, his regiments seeming unreliable. He had urged de Launay to hold firm, but his message had fallen into the hands of the insurgents. In the evening he beat a retreat to Saint-Cloud.

Thus fell the Bastille, through the ineptitude of its governor, the defection of royal troops and the heroic tenacity of a few hundred assailants. The treachery attributed to de Launay confirmed the fear of an aristocratic conspiracy. No one supposed that the Bastille itself was a stake in the struggle, and no one at first thought that its fall would settle the issue. The panic continued during the night of July 14–15. Desèze, who in 1793 was to be defense counsel for the king, and who had been active in organizing the militia, wrote on July 18: "We all expected a fight with regular troops, in which we might be slaughtered." Nevertheless, on the next day the Paris revolution established itself. The electors decided to name a mayor, and their choice fell on Bailly. They offered La Fayette command of the National Guard. La Fayette gave the citizen soldiers, for their insignia, a cockade in the colors of the city of Paris, red and blue, between which he placed white, the color of the king. The tricolor flag, emblem of the Revolution, was a synthesis of the old France and the new.

Of minor importance in itself, the overthrow of the Bastille was yet an event of far-reaching implications, and one which disconcerted the Court. The capital was lost to the king and determined to defend itself. The troops on hand were insufficient to take the city by assault or to surround it, and in any case their loyalty was uncertain. Moreover, the provinces would probably imitate Paris. During the night of July 14–15 the king vacillated between flight and submission. No third course was envisaged by him. Later he admitted to Fersen, the queen's friend, that he had "missed his chance," but at the moment flight seemed unworthy of a king, despite the exhortations of the comte d'Artois.

On July 15 he appeared before the Assembly, protested his good intentions and announced the removal of the troops. On the following day he recalled Necker. On the seventeenth, with fifty deputies, he went to Paris. He met with a dignified but cool reception. At the Hôtel de Ville, Bailly expressed satisfaction that the people had "reconquered" their king. Louis XVI, presented with a national cockade, fastened it to his hat. On his return to Versailles his acceptance of the situation seemed final, and the popular joy burst out in wild acclaim.

But fear remained, for no one concluded that the aristocracy had disarmed. Some French Guards thought they had been poisoned. A rumor spread at Versailles that an underground passage had been dug from the stables of the comte d'Artois to blow up the Assembly. In Paris the committee met with the greatest difficulties in procuring grain. These were attributed to malevolence; riots broke out everywhere, in the market places and along the way of the grain convoys; on the seventeenth a miller was massacred at Saint-Germain-en-Laye, and on the eighteenth a farmer barely escaped the same fate. Destruction of standing crops was daily expected, and on July 26 the Assembly was informed, mistakenly, that in Picardy it had already begun. From all parts of the provinces came disquieting reports of the emigration of aristocrats, preparation by the foreign powers and movements of hired brigands. The comte d'Artois had left France, along with the Condé, Polignac and many other families. A British squadron was said to be cruising off Brest, and there was rumored to be a conspiracy, involving the nobles of

Brittany, to throw open the port to it. The British ambassador protested but convinced no one. The committee searched the approaches to the capital for brigands, and tried to chase vagabonds back to the parishes from which they had come. The whole suburban area, expecting to be infested with vagrants, called out its militia. Local panics appeared at Bougival, Sceaux, Villiers-le-Bel and Pontoise on the seventeenth and eighteenth, at Etampes on the twenty-first. The repercussions were felt in Paris.

The popular victory had not quieted the atmosphere, and the press, now free, added to the excitement by giving out retrospective details on the aristocratic conspiracy, and echoing every rumor that seemed to prove its continuation. Along with fear went a rising will to punish and repress. As early as July 13 Desèze noted talk of "exterminating all nobles." Despite their efforts, neither Bailly nor La Fayette was master of Paris. At the request of the former the electoral districts of the city chose on July 23 a common council of 120 members, which succeeded to the electors; but the district assemblies continued to meet every day, claiming to have to discuss, confirm or reject the policies of the municipal government. In this way, not the laboring class but the lesser bourgeoisie of skilled craftsmen and shopkeepers sought to institute a direct democracy. They too made up most of the new National Guard.

By an unfortunate coincidence, three men were arrested almost simultaneously in the outskirts of the city—Bertier de Sauvigny, intendant of Paris and the Île-de-France, thought to be responsible for the food shortage and the supposed abuses in provisioning; his father-in-law Foullon de Doué, thought to have been designated as an aide to Breteuil in the ministry of July 11; and, lastly, Besenval. Foullon, brought to Paris on July 22, was seized by a mob at the Hôtel de Ville and hanged on the nearest lantern. A few minutes later Bertier appeared and met the same end. Again the heads were cut off and paraded on pikestaffs. Besenval arrived strongly escorted on the thirtieth, and probably would also have perished except for the intervention of Necker, who, reached opportunely near the Swiss frontier, had just reappeared on the scene.

These murders raised strong protest in the Assembly, notably from Lally-Tollendal. A well-known letter of Babeuf shows his horror at seeing the people thus soil its triumph. But it would be wrong to imagine that the revolutionary bourgeoisie was unanimous in its disapproval. "Is this blood then so pure that one should so regret to spill it?" cried Barnave openly in the National Assembly. And Mme. Roland wrote from Beaujolais at the end of the month: "If the National Assembly doesn't put two famous heads on trial, or if our patriotic Deciuses don't strike them down, you're all mad." She, like Barnave, was haunted by the mass idea of an aristocratic plot.

Nevertheless, how could anyone deny, however he may have thought the popular fury justified, that these summary executions had to be ended? Accordingly the idea arose at this time of creating a court and a police power specifically charged with repressing the aristocratic conspiracy. Thus all pretext for tumultuous popular intervention would be taken away, and the security of the Revolution would be better assured than by spasmodic outbursts. On July 23 Duclos-Dufresnoy, a notary of the Rue de Richelieu, in the name of the district of Filles-Saint-Thomas, appeared before the Assembly and proposed the creation of a court of sixty sworn jurymen, one from each district of Paris, and apparently to be elected by the people. It was to be a popular revolutionary tribunal, obviously corresponding to the direct government which the districts were trying to set up in the capital. Barnave likewise, though less explicitly, demanded "legal justice for state crimes," and Prieur a committee to receive denunciations. In the evening session some deputies again brought the matter up, notably Petion, who seems to have backed the idea of having the jurymen elected. The Assembly, in the proclamation to the nation which it adopted, promised to create a committee to receive and verify denunciations concerning the aristocratic plot, and to specify the court to judge the guilty, while reserving the right of prosecution exclusively for itself. But nothing was done until July 28.

On that day, just after appointment of a committee to examine the stream of incoming petitions had been decided upon, du Port insisted that the committee announced on the twenty-third, and which he called a "committee of investigation," should also be established. He had his way; the resulting body was the prototype of the famous Committee of General Security. The Commune of Paris, likewise, on the motion of Brissot, set up a committee of its own, the prototype of the local revolutionary surveillance committees. Meanwhile du Port, in turn, had demanded a "provisional" tribunal for crimes of *lèse-nation*. This question, it was agreed, should be examined by the committee of investigation, which, however, was not appointed until the thirtieth, at the time of the riot in which Besenval almost lost his life. Hoping to save him, the Paris government promised to create a popular tribunal elected by the districts, and Bailly and Semonville appeared before the Assembly to ask an appropriate decree. The Assembly contented itself with reaffirming its decision of the twenty-eighth. At bottom, the majority in the Assembly simply wished to gain time. Some deputies protested, comparing the proposed tribunal to the "extraordinary commissions" with which the old absolutism had been so much reproached. Privately, the representatives of the Commune were strongly condemned. The Commune did not insist. The affair was buried, so thoroughly that history has taken no notice of it.

But the committee of investigation remained, and from July 25 to 27 a revealing debate took place on some letters seized from the baron de Castelnau, which the president of the Assembly had not wished to open without the Assembly's permission. Some held out for the privacy of personal correspondence. Others, Target and Barnave no less than Petion and Robespierre, maintained that the nation had a right to use any methods to expose the aristocratic conspiracy. It was a noble, Gouy d'Arsy, who spoke the deciding words: "In a state of war it is allowable to unseal letters, and . . . we can consider ourselves to be, and are in truth, in a state of war." The Assembly passed to the order of the day, but it is clear that already, a month before adoption of the Declaration of the Rights of Man and the Citizen, the relative character of these rights had been affirmed, and that the theory was already being developed, so often defended by the Committee of Public Safety in the Year Two of the Republic, that in a state of war constitutional guarantees may be suspended.

More than once it has been pointed out, to throw a bad light on the victory of the Third Estate and the memory of July 14, that the second half of July saw the first manifestations of the Terror. This is true beyond question. But the fact can be seen in its true historical significance only when we reconstruct the origin and content of the mass beliefs in which the Terror arose. We then realize that the "aristocratic conspiracy" is one of the keys to the history of the Revolution. It seemed foiled in 1789, and hence the repressive action slackened. But beginning at the end of that year it became a reality, with the essential features that the people had ascribed to it in advance. When extreme fears returned in 1792, with the Prussians and the *émigrés* marching on the soil of France, it was in vain that Danton created the Tribunal of August 17, demanded three years earlier, for the September Massacres broke out none the less. And in 1793, at the moment of supreme peril, the Convention prevented a recurrence of massacre only by giving the Terror an official organization. Fear and its train of murderous passions died away gradually, but only after the victory of the Revolution was consolidated beyond dispute.

CHAPTER 8   *The Municipal*
                   Revolutions
                   in the Provinces

THE dismissal of Necker raised
a lively excitement in the provincial cities, and the reaction
this time, violent and immediate, was unquestionably
spontaneous, for the deputies at Versailles had no time to
intervene, and the government had in any case purposely
suspended the movement of the mails. New addresses poured
in upon the Assembly from all directions. Many were menacing in tone. At Nîmes, for example, on July 20, the citizens
declared "the agents of despotism and promoters of aristocracy to be scoundrels and traitors to the country," and
enjoined upon all men of Nîmes in the army to disobey any
orders they might receive to shed the blood of fellow citizens. Nor was this all. In several cities the insurgents seized
whatever would be of use to the royal authorities in carrying
out the program of the Court, notably the public funds and
the stores of grain and forage. At Le Havre, grain on its way
to Paris was stopped, and hussars, brought from Honfleur,
were forced to go over to the patriot side. Conversely, preparations were made to resist the royal troops and march to
the defense of the National Assembly. Committees were
formed, at Montauban, Bourg, Laval and elsewhere; these in
turn organized a local militia, and in some cases called upon

neighboring towns for aid (as did Château-Gontier) or even upon the peasants, as at Bourg and Machecoul. Serious incidents occurred at Rennes and Dijon. The bourgeoisie of Rennes, on July 16, not content with seizing the public funds and forming themselves into a militia, won part of the garrison to their side and appropriated arms and cannon. The governor, Langeron, called for reinforcements, but the town rebelled on the nineteenth and the rest of the garrison joined the citizens, so that Langeron withdrew from the city. At Dijon on July 15 the governor was arrested and nobles and priests were confined to their homes. This was the first example of detention of suspects.

News of the fall of the Bastille was received from July 16 to 19, according to the distance from Paris. It produced an explosion of enthusiasm and delight. More addresses reached the Assembly, this time of congratulation. Throughout the country there were rejoicings and *Te Deums* and processions carrying the national cockade for presentation to the authorities, who, willingly or not, accepted it and wore it like everyone else. Bonfires were lit in the evening.

In many cities the municipal revolution proceeded without violence. The municipality of the Old Regime simply caved in before the demonstrators. The old municipal authorities merely took a number of notables into their organization, or, as at Bordeaux, disappeared before the electors. Elsewhere they allowed a subsistence committee to be formed. More often, to control the militia, they were obliged to create a "permanent committee" which sooner or later absorbed the entire administration. The movement was invariably characterized by formation of a "national guard," an essential point in the eyes of the bourgeoisie. Worthy of notice is the role played by younger men, who very often organized themselves in distinct companies and sometimes obtained their own representatives on the committee. There were cases also in which regular soldiers fraternized with the citizens and likewise had their own delegates.

But in some places the bulk of the people were unwilling merely to associate themselves with the bourgeoisie. They called on the city authorities to reduce the price of bread, or besieged the town hall with cries of "Bread at two sous!" The town officers might hesitate, or take flight when threatened; riots would then break out, and the homes of officials, grain merchants and wealthy citizens would be pillaged or at least attacked; the militia, or sometimes the garrison, would arrive belatedly and put an end to the disorder. At Valenciennes and at Valence the old town officers were reinstated. More often, as at Lille, Maubeuge or Cherbourg, the old municipality was seen no more, being replaced by a "national" or a "permanent" committee. In such cases the local revolution was complete.

Usually the new municipal body filled itself out by cooptation, or indeed the committee determined its membership on its own authority. These self-appointed notables, in the following weeks, often had to yield to elected persons, but the democratic development was slower and less clearly marked than in Paris. In any case, there was a third category of cities, in which all that happened was the formation of a militia, the powers of the Old Regime remaining intact. In this category were Béziers and all the towns of maritime Flanders, where the old authorities had the prudence to keep down the price of bread on their own initiative.

The provincial revolution thus varied from place to place, and often remained only a halfway movement. But everywhere the town authorities were obliged to accept the orders of the National Assembly only. Almost all the intendants abandoned their posts. In the provinces, as in Paris, the king was deprived of authority. Central authority disappeared at the same time, for each committee or municipality now exercised an uncontrolled and almost absolute power not only in its town but in the parishes of the neighborhood, into which the militia was dispatched to visit suspected châteaux, find and escort grain supplies or put down disturbances. The need of union to preserve the Revolution was strongly felt; towns already exchanged promises of aid and assistance, and regional federations began to form. But the desire was equally strong to set up and jealously defend the most extensive local autonomy. France surged spontaneously in a federation of local units. The National Assembly no doubt enjoyed a prestige which no later assembly was to possess. But each town—and the rural parishes lost no time in freeing themselves in the same way—remained none the less mistress of its own policy, enforcing the decrees of the Assembly with more or less zeal and exactitude, and not rigorously respecting them unless they accorded clearly with local opinion. Autonomy helped undoubtedly to awaken interest in public affairs in the citizens, and to keep local leaders alert and give them initiative. The extraordinary activity of municipal and regional life is one of the characteristic traits of the period. From it the defense of the Revolution profited greatly, for after July 1789 France was covered with a network of committees, all zealous to watch over the aristocrats and undo their machinations.

But the under side of the picture soon became visible. First of all, what did the mass of the city people expect? They expected an abolition of the indirect taxes and a strict control of the trade in grain. Somehow, by force or otherwise, these expectations had to be satisfied. Taxes were ceasing to be collected; the offices of the salt monopoly, the liquor excise and the municipal tolls were often sacked, their accounts destroyed and their hated functionaries put to flight. As for grain, it no longer moved unless accompanied by certificates of security or minutely drawn up letters authorizing its transport, and despite such precautions its passage was often blocked by riots. In the markets, though they were closely regulated, purchases by grain dealers and by commissioners of the large cities excited continual troubles. The scarcity and high price of bread produced rebellions well into the autumn. Whether the issue was taxes or food supplies, the National Guard was always half-hearted in repressing disorder, and in some cases instigated it, a fact not surprising when it is recalled that the guard was made up mainly of craftsmen and shopkeepers who shared in the popular feeling. The National Assembly in a proclamation of August 10 reminded the country that the old taxes remained payable until a new fiscal system should be established, and on August 29 decreed complete internal freedom of the grain trade, only exportation remaining forbidden. But the Assembly preached in the desert.

It is a notable fact that the insurrections and occasional murders (as at Bar-le-Duc and Tours) by which the provincial revolution was marked had as their immediate cause, in almost every case, either poverty or high prices. But this is not to say that the provinces were untroubled by fears of the "aristocratic conspiracy," or that these fears were dissipated by the king's capitulation. Regiments returning from Paris were received in their garrison towns with dismay. Châlons and Verdun refused to take back the Royal German. When Marshal de Broglie tried to set up his headquarters at Sedan he was forced by the crowd to depart. All movement of arms or money was suspected because it might be bound for foreign destinations. Force was used to prevent people from leaving the country: coaches were stopped and searched, and prominent persons such as bishops, nobles and deputies were held until further orders. Foreign intervention was increasingly expected.

In the West, as has been seen, rumor had the English threatening to occupy Brest, in the Southeast the Piedmontese preparing to attack Dauphiny, at Bordeaux the Spaniards due soon to arrive. "Brigands" were seen everywhere, so much so that word spread through the Paris suburbs that vagrants were being driven out of the capital, and similar warnings were heard near all the larger cities. Thus one local panic followed another, at Verneuil and its environs on July 21, at Brives on the twenty-second, at Clamecy on the twenty-ninth. Local revolutionary leaders, convinced that the aristocracy was planning new moves, utilized all such rumors to justify their own actions; and the deputies at Versailles likewise, filled with resentment and suspicion, put their constituents on guard, urged them to vigilance and recommended the formation of local militias. The provincial towns, like Paris, were on the alert; it was the eve of the Great Fear.

PART IV   ⊕   THE PEASANT

REVOLUTION

CHAPTER 9   *The Peasantry*

THERE was scarcely any question of the peasants before July 14. Yet they formed at least three quarters of the population of the kingdom, and we realize today that without their adherence the Revolution could with difficulty have succeeded. Their grievances had been disregarded in the drafting of the bailiwick petitions, or had at best received little emphasis. Their complaints were by no means uppermost among the interests of the National Assembly, in which there were no peasant members. Then suddenly they too revolted, taking their cause into their own hands and delivering a death blow to what was left of the feudal and manorial system. The peasant uprising is one of the most distinctive features of the Revolution in France.

The Peasants and the Land

In 1789 the great majority of the French peasants had been free for many generations, i.e., they could move about and work as they wished, possess property and bring suit in the law courts. Some "serfs" could still be found, principally in Franche-Comté and the Nivernais, but they were no longer really attached to the soil, and in 1779 the king had even abolished the right of pursuit, which had allowed the lord to make good his claims over the serf wherever the latter might go. The main characteristic of serfdom in France was lack of freedom in disposing of goods. The serf was a *mainmortable* or man under a mortmain; if, at his death, he did not have at least one living child residing with him, all his possessions reverted to the lord. In France the serf was far better off than in central and eastern Europe, where the peasantry was left under the nobleman's arbitrary jurisdiction. In France the king's justice protected the rights and person of both serf and free man.

Not only were most French peasants not serfs. Many were landowners, differing in this respect from the peasants of England, who in general had been reduced by the landed aristocracy to the status of wage laborers. The size and number of peasant properties varied greatly from one region to another. They were most extensive in Alsace, Flanders, Limousin, parts of Normandy, the Loire valley, the plains of the Saône and the Garonne and generally throughout southern France more than in the North. In these regions peasants owned from half to three-quarters of the soil. Elsewhere the proportion fell much lower, notably in barren, marshy or forested regions and in the neighborhood of cities. Of the land around Versailles peasant ownership accounted for no more than one or two per cent. Thirty per cent is a probable average for the kingdom as a whole. The remaining land was owned by the clergy (probably a tenth of the kingdom), the nobles (over twice as much) and the bourgeoisie (perhaps a fifth). The clergy was especially wealthy in the North, less so as one went west and south. The nobles seem to have been wealthiest in the North, East and West. Bourgeois ownership of rural land was characteristic of the South.

Yet everywhere there were propertyless peasants. Rarely was the number of these rural proletarians negligible: it has been estimated at about a fifth of family heads in Limousin,

30 to 40 per cent in the Norman woodlands, 70 per cent around Versailles and as high as 75 per cent in maritime Flanders. Some of these unpropertied peasants found land to rent. Ecclesiastics, noblemen and bourgeois seldom exploited their own lands, except in the wine country and in some parts of the South. Instead, they put them in the hands of farmers, or more often of sharecroppers with whom they divided the produce. Moreover, their estates consisted in many small unconnected parcels, which they were glad to lease out separately bit by bit. Hence the laborer could manage to procure a patch for himself, and the peasant owner, for his part, could supplement his own holdings with additional parcels taken on lease. In this way the rural proletariat in the strict sense, or peasants who had no land either by ownership or by leasehold, was substantially reduced while never disappearing entirely. Hence also rural society had as many gradations as society in the cities. The most well to do were the large farmers, who often owned no land themselves. Next came the substantial class, called *laboureurs*, who worked considerable tracts which they owned wholly or in part. They were followed, in downward order, by the small farmer, the sharecropper, the peasant having the use of some land but not enough to live on, the laborer possessing a house and garden plus some small parcel on lease and finally the laborer who had nothing but his hands.

Unfortunately the holdings of the overwhelming majority of the peasants were not large enough to support them and their families. Backward methods of cultivation were in part the cause. In the North and East the village lands were subdivided into countless long and narrow strips, which were grouped in three "fields." One field was sown with winter wheat, one with a spring crop, while the third lay fallow, i.e., uncultivated, each field changing its role from year to year. South of a line running from eastern Normandy to Burgundy and passing by Beauce there were only two fields, of which one always lay fallow. In the West, in Limousin and in the mountains, the cultivated areas, enclosed by hedges, comprised an even smaller fraction of the soil, the remaining land being worked only from time to time, sometimes only one year in ten, sometimes even less often. In any case, triennial or biennial rotation left a third or half the arable soil unproductive. Hence the peasant needed more land than today. In the region later comprised in the department of Nord nine families out of ten had too little to live on. The situation had grown worse since the middle of the eighteenth century, for the population had increased perceptibly, probably by three million. The number of proletarians had risen, while through division of inheritances the shares of property owners had become smaller. There was, therefore, at the end of the Old Regime, an agrarian crisis.

Hence many peasants invaded the commons when the king, in 1764 and 1766, granted exemption from tithes and taxes to persons who cleared new land. Borders of the forests, and open places within them, swarmed with barefoot pioneers who built themselves cabins, cleared what they could and felled timber either for sale or for conversion into charcoal. The marshes likewise hid a wretched population which lived by fishing or cutting peat. Peasant landowners, in the grievance-lists, roundly criticized the nobles and clergy who exploited their own estates directly, and demanded also that the big properties be leased out, not to a few large farmers, but to many small ones. In Picardy and Hainaut, when the owners tried to change farmers, the latter fought back against eviction, even to the point of arson and murder. It is therefore not surprising to find some parishes asking for alienation of the crown lands and even of part of the property of the clergy. But it is characteristic of the time that the property of individuals was never questioned. At the height of the Terror, when the property of *émigrés* and of persons condemned for political offenses was sold, and when it was decided also to confiscate the property of mere suspects, the principle was always that of penalizing enemies of the country. Nobles who stayed in France, and remained peaceable, never at any time during the Revolution saw their property threatened. This was because the land, when it was not the property of the peasants, was already in their hands on leasehold terms. Farm rentals, it is true, had almost doubled during the eighteenth century, while prices had gone up on the average not more than sixty-five per cent. Sharecropping too had become less favorable to the peasant; in general, the owner still took only half the crop or half the increment of livestock, but he increasingly imposed obligations of many kinds and even a supplemental payment in cash, especially in cases where sharing arrangements were managed through a "farmer-general," who found it to his advantage to bring pressure on the croppers. There was much bitter complaint on this score in Bourbonnais, Nivernais and Beaujolais. Nevertheless, despite all these grievances, the farmer or sharecropper would have nothing to gain by exchanging his leased holdings for the tiny parcel which a general redistribution of property would procure for him. And it is obvious that those peasants who already owned property would not have favored any such redistribution.

Taxes, Tithes, Fees, Dues

Keeping in mind that the agrarian crisis was real and pressing, we must recognize that there was only one matter on which the whole rural population could unanimously agree—namely, the obligations imposed by the king and the aristocracy.

The peasant was almost alone in paying the *taille* and drawing lots for militia service. He alone was held for road

134 THE PEASANT REVOLUTION

work and for aid in military transportation. From him came most of the proceeds of the poll-tax and the twentieth-taxes. Yet it was the indirect taxes that he detested the most, especially the government salt monopoly, which held the price of salt as high as thirteen sous a pound in a large part of the kingdom. The royal demands had steadily risen during the eighteenth century, and the parish grievance-lists of 1789 invariably complained of them, but we cannot say, in view of the general rise in the price level, whether they actually took a greater part of the national income in 1789 than a half century before. Probably they did. In Wallon Flanders, a region having Provincial Estates and hence getting off fairly lightly, the increase in direct taxes in the reign of Louis XVI alone has been estimated at twenty-eight per cent. The peasants, while critical of the bourgeois, observing that commercial wealth paid less than its proper share, were most especially aroused to a state of fury by the privileges of the aristocracy.

The royal taxation, a relatively new burden superimposed on the payments made from time immemorial to the aristocracy, undoubtedly had the indirect consequence of making these payments far more hateful. To the clergy was due the tithe, variable in amount but almost always less than a tenth, levied on the "great" grains, wheat, rye, oats and barley (the "great tithe"), and on other grains and vegetables and fruits (the "small tithe"), and on a few animal products. From the peasant grievance-lists it is evident that the tithe would have been more willingly paid if the proceeds, instead of going in most cases to bishops, abbeys or chapters, or even to lay lords to whom the tithe might be "subinfeudated" (the parish priest receiving the small tithe at most), had been used, as they should have been, to support public worship, the parish church and parsonage and above all the poor. But the peasant, after paying the tithe, saw most of the expense for such purposes still falling upon himself. In addition the tithe had all the disadvantages of a levy collected in kind. The tithe owner had to come and take it away himself; if he delayed, the whole crop might suffer from bad weather; the peasant was deprived of straw, a material necessary to manure, and the only one known to him. The tithe also blocked the progress of land clearance and of new methods of cultivation. Since it was collected in kind, a rise in prices made it more profitable to the collector; in 1789 the gross product was thought to be worth 120,000,000 livres. The profit was greatest in times of scarcity, at the cost of the peasant's very subsistence; and in any case, at all times, the tithe collector seemed a food hoarder by his very nature.

What there was left of feudalism was even more disliked. The strictly feudal should be distinguished from the manorial. From the feudal point of view land consisted of fiefs, depending one upon another and all finally upon the king. Fiefs were subject to a law of their own, of which the law of primogeniture is the best known; and with each change of owner the suzerain required the vassal to make due acknowledgment, submit a survey of the estate and pay a fee. Unless the peasant had bought a fief, which was rare at least in the North, this system did not concern him. If he had bought a fief he paid the king, as did the bourgeois in the same circumstances, a special fee called the *franc-fief*.

Among owners of fiefs some were seigneurs or manorial lords over the people settled on their lands. The essential characteristic of manorial lordship was justice, high and low. High justice carried the right to condemn to death, which however was a pure form, since every capital sentence had to be approved by a Parlement. A lord exercising high justice retained the right to conduct criminal proceedings and operate police courts, in which, however, he took little interest since they produced no income. In 1772 the king authorized lords to free themselves of expense in such matters by simply turning over the accused to the royal courts. On the other hand, civil cases and low justice were of great value. Low justice included the rural police power and the right to adjudicate differences relating to manorial payments. The latter was valuable to the lord in that, through his judges, he decided in his own case. And even had his right of justice ceased to be "useful," the lord would have defended it jealously, for it was the symbol of his social superiority, conveying various honorary prerogatives, such as a private pew with his coat of arms, the right to present holy water or consecrated bread, to be buried in the church choir, to maintain a gallows as the sign of justice and to receive from the peasants certain personal services, sometimes humiliating, which signified their dependent status.

On high or low justice, moreover, the lawyers made a number of remunerative other rights depend—exclusive rights of hunting and fishing, of keeping pigeon houses and rabbit warrens, the levying of market tolls and road and river tolls, control over weights and measures, obligations of watch and ward at the manor house, personal services for the lord and, perhaps most important of all, the right of *ban*. This was the right to promulgate orders on such matters as the opening of the harvest or vintage season or the regulation of taverns. From the right of *ban* was derived the *ban* of wines, which reserved to the lord, for a certain period, the exclusive right to sell new wine. From it too came the *banalités* or exclusive right to maintain a mill, oven or wine press, lucrative monopolies which the lord farmed out for his own profit. Justice carried with it also property in the roads except for the king's highways, and consequently the so-called planting right, much used in the eighteenth century in some provinces such as Flanders, Artois and

Anjou to embellish the public highways with trees, though at the cost of encroaching on peasant farmlands. Finally, to end the list, it was because of the lord's powers of justice that personal services or payments in money or in kind, variously called *tailles, fouages,* etc., were exacted in many villages from every person domiciled therein.

These strictly seignorial rights, or rights of lordship, should be distinguished from the "real" rights, so called because they were deemed to fall not on persons but on land. All owners of fiefs, whether lords or not, enjoyed such "real" rights. Fief owners did not exploit their own land except for the part called the "domain," which consisted in the manor house and park, a bit of meadow or forest and the areas leased out to sharecroppers and to tenant farmers. The rest of the fief was in the hands of the peasants or "holders," who enjoyed rights of inheritance in their holdings and could also dispose of them freely—these were the peasant proprietors mentioned above. But the master of the fief none the less retained over these holdings the right of "direct" or "eminent" property. He was supposed by the law to have granted the holding to the peasant under a perpetual title, in return for payments fixed once and for all in amount, and which could not be compounded or bought up without his consent. These payments were of two types. Some were due annually; they were called *cens* or quitrents, and might consist in a sum of money, normally very small, or in a stated amount of produce, and in this case far more valuable in view of the rise of prices. On cultivated lands the quitrent in kind became in effect a sort of tithe, levied according to a uniform scale and generally known in the North as the *champart* or *terrage,* in the South as the *agrier* or *tasque.* "Real" payments of the second type were occasional, falling due in the event of transfer by inheritance or sale. These were called *lods et ventes* and were very onerous, reaching at least an eighth and sometimes even a half of the value of the holding. As for the serfs, they were subject in addition to the particular obligations already mentioned.

Increasing Pressures

During the eighteenth century the demands of manorial lords, like those of the king, had become more burdensome for the peasants. Since the system had been criticized by the philosophers and economists, manorial lords thought it necessary to reaffirm their rights by frequently renewing the manor rolls in which they were written down and by requiring exact payment. Increasingly they farmed out their rights to professional collectors, who were inexorable in their work, reviving and enforcing almost obsolete obligations, if indeed not broadening them in a way that was positively an abuse. Where claims were contested, the manorial courts and the Parlements always decided against the peasants. But what exasperated the rural people, since they had in any case too little land for a livelihood, was the encroachment on their collective rights, on which their existence depended.

Land in fallow, constituting a half or third of the arable soil, together with land tilled only at long intervals, was considered to be common land, to which all persons, or at least all proprietors, might send their livestock to graze. Cultivated fields became part of the common patrimony after the harvest, and meadows after the first or in any case the second mowing; here, once the crops were in, the village community enjoyed the right of "vacant pasture." Often the village had a common herdsman who assembled all the animals of the neighborhood. This is why the fields remained "open." Owners were indeed authorized by custom (except in the three-field regions) to enclose their property with a fence or wall, in order to keep out other than their own animals; but they seldom employed this right because enclosure was expensive and above all because it infuriated the peasants. The common lands, which remained extremely extensive, especially in the mountains and in the West, constituted an important resource to the poor. In the forests the peasant could pasture his stock, gather dead wood and cut trees, either to keep himself warm or to build or repair his house or his agricultural implements. On cultivated land, after the harvest, he had the right of "gleaning" and of cutting stubble, which the almost universal use of the sickle left very high. These collective rights were condemned by economists as obstacles to agricultural improvement. The great landowners, almost all belonging to the aristocracy, were of the same opinion. Forests, except for common wood lots, had been gradually closed to the peasants since the wood and water ordinance promulgated by Colbert in 1669. During the second half of the eighteenth century, in certain provinces, the Crown authorized enclosure and the breakup of commons. It was mainly the aristocracy that benefited. Lords denied the right of vacant pasture on their own lands, while continuing to send their herds on to lands belonging to peasants. As for the commons, in which peasant holders had only a right of use, the jurists adjudged the right of "eminent" property to belong to the manorial lords, who consequently did not hesitate to break them up and put them into cultivation for their own profit. When commons were partitioned among individual owners the lord took a third, by the right of *triage*.

Numerous are the peasant grievance-lists which complain, and complain bitterly, of these constant encroachments, as of the generally growing exactions of the feudal class. They insist on the damage done to agriculture by the hunting rights, the dovecotes and the rabbit warrens in the absence of proper regulation and of any recourse. Payments in kind were subjected to the same criticism as was the tithe. The petitions call attention to the crushing weight of all these dues taken together, finding it heavier than the parallel burden of the royal taxes. More rare are the petitions which propose remedies, such as suppression of certain rights considered particularly repugnant, or authorization to buy up the manorial dues. The principle of the system is never questioned, but we must note that the peasants did not express all that was on their minds, and that on the matter of manorial rights the bourgeois who assumed leadership over them were often reticent in their opinions, since manorial rights were a form of property, which some bourgeois had themselves purchased, and in which others had an interest as judges or agents for the manorial lords. Still, the deeper workings of the peasant mind can be seen in one way, when their petitions demand that the original document specifying payments in return for holdings be produced, and that in its absence such payments be brought to an end. The peasant proprietor, it is clear, thought himself the only legitimate owner of his land, and considered the payments due the lord, unless there was proof to the contrary, to have originated in nothing but violence. In some cases peasant rancor against lordly "bloodsuckers" did in fact express itself plainly.

Yet we must guard against supposing that the manorial regime was the same from one end of the kingdom to the other, or that all parishes labored under the same burdens. Very oppressive in some provinces such as Brittany and Franche-Comté, it was comparatively light in others such as maritime Flanders. On this as on other points France was infinitely diversified. Nor did all peasants have the same interest in abolition of the tithe and manorial dues, from which the landowners among the peasants would benefit chiefly. Yet that these obligations, far more than the royal taxes, were execrated unanimously by the whole peasantry cannot be doubted and was to be proved by experience. Against the aristocracy the peasants had far more substantial grievances than did the people of the cities, and it is natural therefore that they took it upon themselves to deal the blow by which the aristocracy was laid low.

CHAPTER 10   *The Agrarian Revolts and the Great Fear*

THE hatred of the peasants for the lords was not a thing of yesterday. The history of France abounds in *jacqueries*. In the eighteenth century the collection of manorial dues more than once led to troubles, and in particular engendered innumerable lawsuits which the peasants sustained with incredible tenacity. Yet if they were brought to a state of general rebellion in 1789 one reason is to be found in the convocation of the Estates-General. One can hardly exaggerate the echoes produced by this event in the countryside. On hearing of it the peasants concluded that, if the king invited them to set forth their grievances, it was because he meant to give them satisfaction—and that, if things were going badly, it was because they had too much to pay, to the king himself of course, but above all to the tithe owner and the manorial lord. In their eyes the king's intention, never doubtful, was the same as the accomplished fact; in any case, if they anticipated a little, they would please him. The bailiwick lieutenant of Saumur observed, as the most unsettling feature of convocation of the Estates, that the electoral assemblies of the parishes thought themselves invested with sovereign authority, and that the rustics believed themselves already rid of the manorial dues. Cries of alarm rose everywhere in the kingdom in the course of the spring: the peasants were declaring their intention to make no payments at the coming harvest. Class solidarity asserted itself strongly. During the disturbances at Chatou the peasants took aside one of their number who seemed suspect, demanded of him, "Are you for the Third Estate?" and when he gave a negative answer told him, "Then we'll give you the idea!" The agrarian insurrections, more even than those of the cities, were genuine mass movements.

At the same time the idea of an "aristocratic conspiracy" grew up and rooted itself even more strongly than in the bourgeois, for the peasants knew by centuries of experience that in the eyes of the lord the manorial dues were untouchable—his social superiority depending on them as well as his income. That the lord would make every effort to deceive the "good king"; that if he failed in this he would take up arms to crush the Third Estate—all this seemed obvious and inevitable to the peasants. The inaction of the Estates-General and their silence on matters of concern to the peasants were attributed to an aristocratic conspiracy. When news came of the resort to force, what doubt could there be? And when it was learned that the king, visiting his insurgent capital, had given his approval to the resistance which had blocked the aristocrats, what reservations could any longer be felt? During the ensuing revolts the peasants insisted that they were executing the king's will. Smuggled orders circulated among them, ostensibly emanating from the king.

The towns, and hence the bourgeoisie, certainly contributed to the formation and spread of this collective state of mind. Many relations, as has been seen, joined the townsmen and rural people. The market places were the main centers of contagion, for the peasant went to market at least once a week, and it is thus that he gathered news, came to share ideas with the town population and found in the urban uprisings a signal for his own revolt.

Yet the same observation must be made of the country as of the towns. The peasant rising would be inconceivable without the excitement produced by the calling of the Estates-General. But it is undeniable also that the economic crisis contributed powerfully to it, and reinforced also the idea of an aristocratic plot. The rural masses suffered cruelly from food shortages, contrary to what might be supposed, for most peasants raised too little to subsist on, and when the harvest was bad the number of those in want increased perceptibly as the year went on. They would go to make purchases at the neighboring market, become involved in the disturbances there and on returning spread trouble and a sense of insecurity through their home parishes. In the open country they would stop shipments of food without hesitation, so that during the summer of 1789 disorder became universal. As for the causes and possible remedies for the problem, they held the same views as the small people of the towns. Regulation was their panacea, the hoarder their enemy.

Scarcity aggravated the effects of rural unemployment, an endemic evil. The day laborer had difficulty in finding work over the winter. When crops were poor he had the same difficulty in the warm season, since the farmers then hired as few hands as possible, finding it hard to feed them. Moreover the business depression, due in part to the hard times in the country, reacted unfavorably on the rural situation because a great many peasants, under the system of domestic industry, supplemented their incomes by working for city merchants. Unemployment and scarcity multiplied the number of beggars, too numerous in the best of times. They were even more dreaded by the peasant than by the townsman, for if he refused their demands he was far more exposed to their revenge, and might find his trees cut down, his cattle mutilated or his barns or haystacks put to the torch. In the spring of 1789 bands of beggars appeared everywhere, going from farm to farm, day and night, spreading threats. At no time was the peasant free from the "fear of brigands"; now he was terrified beyond measure, for they might destroy the crops while still unripe. The authorities recognized the danger, and reluctantly allowed and even ordered the peasants to arm themselves and maintain guards. Local panics broke out here and there well before July 14. It was these panics that put the towns on the alert. Like the bourgeois, the peasants suspected the aristocracy of keeping both brigands and foreign troops in its pay. This supposed collusion was what spread the "fear of brigands" to the nation as a whole, giving it a social and political significance.

Hence the economic crisis had revolutionary consequences in two ways. On the one hand it enflamed the peasants by turning them against the tithe owners and lords who took away part of their livelihood through the manorial dues. On the other hand, by multiplying the number of those in want, it generalized a sense of insecurity which in the end was blamed on a conspiracy of the aristocrats.

The Agrarian Revolts

Just as fear in no sense dated from July 14, so it would be wrong to imagine that the peasant waited for the example of the capital to revolt. The example of the nearest town was sufficient, and even this was by no means indispensable. At the end of March the high price of bread led to popular uprisings at Toulon and Marseilles, from which agitation spread immediately to all upper Provence. The villages of the Avance Valley, in the region of Gap, rose in insurrection against their lord on April 20. On May 6 a riot broke out at Cambrai; the whole Cambrésis was instantly aflame; the contagion spread to Picardy. Near Paris and Versailles the peasants organized a systematic extermination of game, pillaged the forests and fired on the wardens.

But it need hardly be said that the great commotion of July 14 had a decisive influence. Four insurrections followed from it. One took place in Normandy, where market riots repeatedly broke out north of Perche, and at Falaise on July 17 and 18; a few days later the château-at Caen was occupied by patriots; for six days beginning July 22 a peasant uprising spread from south of Falaise westward to Noireau and southward to Mayenne and beyond. In the North, Picardy and Cambrésis were unable to rise, since troops were stationed there, but abbeys in the Scarpe valley and south of the Sambre were attacked. Far more violent was the rising in Franche-Comté. On July 19 at the manor house of Quincey near Vesoul the peasants were taking advantage of the Sunday to celebrate the fall of the Bastille. The lord having already fled, his steward received them and invited them to drink. That evening, the wine having run out, one convivial visitor, exploring a cellar, ignited a barrel of powder that happened to be stored there. Several were killed or injured in the explosion. There were cries of treachery, and the incident resounded throughout France and even in the Assembly. The next day the manor house went up in flames, and in the following days thirty others on both sides of the Doubs were burned. Around Belfort order was maintained by the garrison. But beyond, by a kind of reaction, a new center of agitation developed in Upper Alsace between July 25 and 30. The scene of the fourth insurrection was Mâconnais, where on July 26 a revolt broke out at Ige. On the next day the whole district was aroused, burning and devastating the manor houses. Attacks on the manor house at Cormatin and the abbey at Cluny were unsuccessful, but the movement continued to spread southward as far as Beaujolais.

These disturbances were all aimed against the aristocracy. One of the chief concerns of the peasants was to force a renunciation of the manorial dues, and above all to burn the archives which authorized their payment. Violence against persons was rare, and though writers have talked of murders the documents reveal none. Very apparent, on the other hand, is the peasant's hostility to all the innovations that threatened his existence. The insurgents pulled down walls and fences, restored the practice of vacant pasture, occupied their lost commons and invaded the forests. Hence the bourgeois was not spared, and even the larger farmers were sometimes molested and obliged to make concessions. In Alsace the Jews in particular suffered. There were signs of local reconciliation between bourgeoisie and nobility, between town committees and authorities of the Old Regime. These were especially noticeable in Mâconnais, where parties of militia patrolled the villages to restore order, and where the committees of Tournus, Cluny and Mâcon organized special courts and called on the old provosts' courts to take action—thirty-three insurrectionists were hanged. But no defense was possible against the peasant's passive resistance to collection of tithes or *champarts* on the current crops. Those paid who wanted to. Moreover, almost simultaneously, the Great Fear was gathering irresistible force.

The Great Fear

The Great Fear originated in local panics, of which two were closely related to the political crisis: at Nantes on July 29 a rumor spread that dragoons were arriving; at Visargent near Lons-le-Saunier, on July 23, certain members of the new national guard, proceeding to a manor house to conduct a search, were mistaken at a distance for brigands, the more easily since revolt was raging in Franche-Comté at the moment. In other places the fear of vagrants, born of social and economic conditions, was an important cause. On July 24, south of Romilly in Champagne, the mere seeing of some people coming out of a forest produced a local terror. At Estrées-Saint-Denis, not far from Clermont in Beauvaisis, on the twenty-sixth, a group of harvesters took alarm for the same reason. The same occurred at Ruffec on the twenty-eighth, and probably the fear in Maine arose in the same way from the neighborhood of the forest of Montmirail. When we remember that the forests then sheltered a numerous population of woodcutters and charcoal burners, a half savage and much dreaded race, it is not surprising to find such incidents playing an important role in the circumstances.

Local panics had sometimes in the past spread remarkably far. The characteristic of the Great Fear is that the six panics mentioned above, which may be called the original ones, set up numerous currents of which some can be traced for hundreds of miles, and which moreover branched out so as to cover entire provinces. In Languedoc and Guyenne in the year 1703, in western Normandy in 1848, in England after the revolution of 1688, there were panics which spread for great distances. But none of these compared with the Great Fear of 1789 which reached throughout the greater part of France. The panic originating at Estrées-Saint-Denis spread north to Flanders, to the sea between Bray and the Somme and toward the south as far as Paris and the Marne Valley. The one starting south of Romilly, in the parish of Maizières-la-Grande, extended north to Châlons, reached Gatinais in the west and descended the valley of the Seine, skirting Paris on the south, traveled through Burgundy to Dijon and went up the Allier into Auvergne. From eastern Maine it passed through that province and into Brittany, alarmed Normandy from Caen to the Seine and moved toward the Loire to a point between Blois and Tours. The panic of Nantes was limited to Poitou. But the one which began in Franche-Comté went as far as Provence, and the Ruffec panic not only reached the Pyrenees but also embraced most of the Massif Central.

The carriers of the panic were people of all conditions. Fugitives explained their fright by enlarging on each other's stories, and these included bourgeois, priests and monks; postal couriers added to the confusion; then many people sent servants to warn their friends; and village curates, local officials and gentry put one another on guard. Even the government subdelegates and mounted constabulary were no exception; they too took the same initiative. The terrors spread because there was no means of verification and because unbelievers easily became suspects. Contrariwise, those regions which the Great Fear never struck probably owed their immunity to the cool behavior of persons who remain unknown.

Rumors of the approach of "brigands" provoked new outbursts of panic, later called "warning panics," which gave a renewed impulse to the propagation of terror. It is these that are remembered in peasant tradition, though in a fragmentary form that makes the whole phenomenon inexplicable. As the wave advanced, the smallest incident coming after it revived the excitement, and these "relays" made the fear rebound in all directions. In Dauphiny the peasants, already assembled in terror of burning, rose up and themselves burned and devastated the manor houses. It was this formidable "relay" that carried the fear from Franche-Comté to the Mediterranean.

Such spread is to be explained by the fact that fear of "brigands" was an old and familiar sentiment in the countryside, and by the political and social conflict which gave birth to the fear of an aristocratic conspiracy of which the "brigands" this time were thought to be instruments.

All contemporaries, after noting that the "brigands" were a myth, concluded that the panic had been sown purposely with no other purpose than to cause trouble. The revolutionaries asserted that the nobles used it as a means of unloosing anarchy and making government impossible, but since the Great Fear turned against the nobles themselves this theory had little success. The aristocracy, for their part, were persuaded that the revolutionaries were the culprits, intending to raise up and arm a people who asked only to remain neutral and at peace. It is still repeated today that the fear was disseminated by mysterious messengers and broke out everywhere on the same day and almost at the same hour. In reality the Great Fear was not universal. Brittany, lower Languedoc, Lorraine, Alsace, Hainaut and Caux never knew it, nor, significantly enough, did those neighborhoods where the peasants had been in insurrection not long before. Nor did it by any means begin everywhere on the same day, but rather expanded by successive impulses from July 20 to August 6. And we can often know by documentary evidence the identity of those who spread it.

It is indisputable that the Great Fear, very improperly named, aroused a strong defensive reaction and brought the peasants to arms, that in Dauphiny it precipitated an agrarian revolt, that everywhere it reinforced sentiments against the aristocracy and that in consequence of it two nobles were murdered at Ballon near Mans and another at Pouzin in Vivarais. But if the panic did remarkably stimulate the insurrection of the peasants, it did not cause it, for they had already risen.

PART V ⊕ THE RIGHTS OF
MAN AND CITIZEN

CHAPTER 11

The Problem
of the Privileges

Rights versus Privileges

WHILE POPULAR revolution
spread, the debates in the National Assembly went on without decisive results. Deputations and addresses flowed in,
and from time to time there were inconclusive discussions
on the restoration of order. The committee on the constitution, appointed on July 14, examined the multiplying proposals both for a constitution and for a declaration of rights.
Not only La Fayette, but also Sieyès, Target, Mounier and others submitted projects for the latter. On July 27 Champion de
Cicé and Mounier brought in the committee's first reports,
and Clermont-Tonnerre added a summary of the grievance-
lists on the subject. The discussion turned on whether such a
declaration was opportune. Most of the patriots warmly took
the affirmative, together with the liberal nobles, pointing to
the example of the Americans and in particular alleging that,
as a means of instructing the people in the principles of the
new order, it was essential to draw up what Barnave called a
"national catechism." The negative was upheld not only by
the privileged but also by some deputies of the Third,
notably Biauzat of Clermont-Ferrand. Though some denied
the existence of natural rights, recognizing only positive

rights as created by law, the great majority of the opposition avoided such underlying philosophy. While natural rights undoubtedly existed, they held, they had necessarily to be delimited by law, and if they were formulated in general philosophical terms the people might later invoke them to question the limits set by the Assembly. It seemed best to this group not to come to a declaration until the constitution was finished, so that the two could be made to harmonize with each other; such especially was Mirabeau's opinion. The matter was settled on the morning of August 4, when the Assembly resolved to begin its work with a Declaration of the Rights of Man and the Citizen.

Only arguments of a general nature, political or philosophical, without immediate application, were advanced during these sessions, so that critics of the debates have often talked as if they went on in an academy of public law. No allusion was made to the privileges or the division of Frenchmen into three orders, none to the royal prerogative, none except in a speech by Malouet to the danger that a declaration of rights might someday be turned against the domination of the bourgeoisie. Yet each speaker had in mind, determining his attitude, some one of these considerations. For the majority of the Assembly the abolition of orders and privileges was naturally the heart of the affair.

The uniting of the three orders in the Assembly had not meant the disappearance of orders as such, any more than did a resolution passed by a minority of the clergy on July 16 to abandon its privileges of taxation, an example which it may be remarked the nobility had not yet officially imitated. On July 8, when the binding mandates were dissolved, a gentleman cried out that the orders were thereby annihilated— showing that they were not yet considered to have been suppressed. As late as August 10 the marquis de Thiboutot, deputy from Caux, undertook to read a speech defending the special law of fiefs and the honorific prerogatives of manorial lords, and asserting that the nobility intended to maintain "the distinctions that characterized it," and would not ratify the abandonment of privileges agreed to by some of its number. Champion de Cicé and Clermont-Tonnerre had spoken on July 27 of creating an upper house, leaving it an open question whether this house might not be monopolized by the two privileged orders.

This is why the aristocrats wished to postpone a declaration. If equality of rights was proclaimed it would be invoked to assimilate them to the rest of the nation. If not, they might succeed in preserving some of their privileges. On July 29, while the rules of procedure of the Assembly were under discussion, a lively debate on the definition of a majority revealed what was in their minds. In place of a simple majority the bishop of Chartres demanded that a two-thirds majority be required for the abolition "of ancient and established laws"; in this event the nobility might hope, putting aside the question of tax exemptions, to gather slightly over three hundred votes against abolition of orders and privileges. As discussion of the principle of a declaration was prolonged, the patriot party grew impatient, convinced that their opponents were in reality using obstructionist tactics.

Nor was this all, for it was not forgotten that since provinces and towns had privileges also, the aristocracy would not be without secret supporters within the Third Estate itself. "Persuaded as we were," wrote Parisot, deputy from Bar-sur-Seine, on the morning of August 5, "that the nobility and clergy were only trying to delay matters and do nothing . . . we felt that as long as the two privileged classes had any privileges whatsoever private interests would overrule the general good." But to submit the abolition of orders and privileges to a regular deliberation would merely reopen the way to obstructionism and unavowed coalitions.

After adjournment at about eleven P.M. on August 3, writes Parisot, "we, that is, about a hundred of us, held a special committee meeting which lasted most of the night." That the Breton Club is here referred to cannot be doubted. It was resolved, he adds, "to use *a kind of magic* by which, calling a truce on the constitutional question, we would obliterate the privileges of classes, provinces, towns and corporations. With this intention we entered the hall yesterday [August 4] at five o'clock. Only our committee was in the secret." The night of the fourth of August was thus the result of a parliamentary maneuver to obtain the most important vote of the revolutionary period by surprise, probably in the hope that many of the opposition would not take the trouble to attend an evening session.

But Parisot does not tell all, and the abolition of privileges was not the sole aim of the "magic."

Insurrection and Turmoil

The popular uprising was perplexing to many patriots. It had saved them and they could not dream of condemning it. On the contrary, they justified it, arguing that after the juridical revolution had restored the people to its sovereignty, and after the king and aristocracy had tried to rob them of their gains by violence, the intervention of the masses and the use of force against force had secured the triumph of right and law. Hence the fourteenth of July was already a sacred revolution. But, thought the patriots, since the Assembly represented the people, the people should restrict themselves to making sure that the Assembly was respected, and should then quietly await such reforms and lawful procedures as the Assembly might judge suitable to decree. But this was far from being the actual state of affairs, and on July 20 and again on the twenty-third Lally-Tollendal raised the alarm.

Everywhere and at every moment public order was dissolving. Summary reprisals had led to bloodshed in town and country. Châteaux and private homes had been burned or looted. The life and property of citizens were unsafe. The people were not waiting upon deliberations of the Assembly to realize their desires; in this respect, the agrarian revolt was especially decisive and revealing. For feudal property, no doubt, there would be no place in the new society, but the bourgeoisie none the less could not approve of its abolition except by legal methods and with compensation, lest a dangerous precedent for other forms of property be set. Moreover, it was only too clear that popular feeling was against economic freedom, destined to be a cornerstone of the coming regime. The populace was demanding definite return to regulation of the grain trade. The traditional economic policy, with all its confining restrictions, was what the peasants showed themselves attached to. Between the bourgeoisie and the rural masses the schism on this matter was radical.

Was it then necessary to call on the army, i.e., the king, to restore the people to submission? The patriots could not make up their minds, and their equivocal position lent strength to the king's abortive moves. The monarch was showered with praise; that he was now in agreement with the Assembly was advertised as certain; and such argument was indeed necessary to reassure the timid and remove all pretext for foreign intervention. Yet everyone wondered whether the Court, at the first favorable moment, would not renew its offensive. The revolutionaries kept suspicion alive in the minds of the least prejudiced by daily denunciations of the "aristocratic conspiracy" as a continuing menace. How could the king be invited to disarm the people? The Assembly would immediately be at his mercy, and this time with no recourse. Several deputies let this be understood clearly in coming to the defense of the "rebels"—and not only Robespierre but men like Barnave also—nor did anyone dare deny what was so evident.

In the towns a solution seemed to be developing in the creation of the national guard, for the Assembly imagined that the artisans and shopkeepers, without whom the citizen militia would be small indeed, did not belong to the "Populace" whose excesses it so deplored. The inability of the guard to restore free movement of grain soon ended this delusion. As for the peasants, it was impossible to be so optimistic. They could be put down only by giving a free hand to the army and the provosts' courts.

Meanwhile on August 3 the committee could think of nothing except to recommend a proclamation—the Assembly would simply instruct the authorities to restore order and the people to continue payment to taxes, tithes and manorial dues. Even this was postponed. "Unjust obligations," cried one deputy, "founded for the most part on violence and force, can never be called legitimate obligations! There is no use talking of feudal dues; the country people expect their suppression, demand it in their petitions, and would simply be irritated by any such proclamation."

The alternative, if force was not to be used, was to give satisfaction to the peasants. The tithe presented no difficulty in principle because it could be regarded as a species of tax; the objection was that, for the support of public worship, it would have to be replaced by a tax which would fall upon everybody, while suppression of the tithe would be profitable only to proprietors of land. As for "feudalism," a speaker on August 3 had implicitly disposed of the argument that its abolition would undermine all property: the feudal rights, he declared, were not like other kinds of property, having mainly arisen as usurpations to the detriment of public authority; and in any case many parish petitions had demanded that manorial lords submit their claims for verification, and especially that they justify the quitrents and other "real" dues by producing the original documents by which they had granted land to the peasants. Here again the aristocracy found much silent support, for many bourgeois were owners of manors or fiefs, or were managers, middlemen or lawyers for manorial lords. But the main obstacle was political. The Revolution had triumphed through the support of parish clergy and liberal nobles. Would it not be imprudent to break with them by despoiling them, against their will, of the tithe and the manorial rights? Target in his proposal for a declaration of rights suggested, like many others, a plan used by the king of Sardinia in 1770, that the feudal rights be bought out with a stipulation that "property rights whose exercise is harmful to the body politic may be annulled only with compensation of at least equal value." But strong resistance and a thousand objections were to be foreseen, leading to endless discussion and inextricable confusion.

Now if ever was the time to resort to the "magic" of which Parisot spoke. The expedient was hit upon of giving the initiative to a liberal nobleman, the duc d'Aiguillon, one of the greatest landowners of France. Much might be expected from such a move: disarray among the aristocrats, emulation among liberal nobles and prelates, a moral obligation upon the recalcitrant of the Third Estate to show themselves no less generous than the privileged. Later, in 1791, the marquis de Ferrières, in denouncing it, did homage to "the art with which the session of the evening of August 4 was planned." The leaders of the revolutionary bourgeoisie, with consummate statesmanly skill, knew how to force their majority to give up private interests and think of the national community at least for a few hours.

The Night of August 4

On Tuesday evening, August 4, the Assembly met to hear Target read the proclamation decided upon in principle the day before. He had hardly ceased speaking when the vicomte de Noailles mounted the tribune. As La Fayette's brother-in-law he was surely in the secret, and it is possible that he intended, by anticipating the duc d'Aiguillon, to do something spectacular by which to be remembered; but as a younger son without fortune of his own he was open to the charge of giving away what he did not possess, and so upsetting the whole plan. The deputies wished, he said, to quiet the popular effervescence, but could they do so without satisfying the peasant communities? "It is not a constitution that the peasants want; this desire was expressed by them only when they got to the bailiwicks. What have they in fact requested? That excise taxes be suppressed; that subdelegates be abolished; that manorial dues be lightened or commuted. The villages for over three months have seen their representatives occupied with what we call and in fact is the public welfare, but to them the public welfare means the kind of welfare that they want and hope fervently to obtain. In all the differences which have divided the representatives of the nation the country people see only one difference—between those whom they recognize as their friends working for their greater happiness, and powerful persons who oppose them. And what is the consequence? They have thought themselves bound to take arms against the use of force, and today they are running entirely unchecked." This was an excellent summary of the psychology of the peasants and the cause of the agrarian insurrections. Noailles consequently proposed that the Assembly, before launching its proclamation, decree equality of taxation and redemption of manorial dues by money payments, except that compulsory labor services, personal mortmain or serfdom and all other personal "servitudes" should disappear without compensation.

The duc d'Aiguillon immediately took up these proposals, suggesting amendments. He justified at length the principle of monetary redemption. "We should face the fact that the rights in question are a form of property and that all property is sacred. But they are burdensome to the people, and all agree on the continual hardship which they cause. . . . We can hardly ask a renunciation pure and simple of the manorial rights. . . . Equity prevents our demanding the surrender of any property without just indemnity to the owner who foregoes his own convenience for the public advantage." He moved that redemption be required without exception.

It may be that d'Aiguillon interpreted the views of the Breton Club more faithfully than Noailles. But the event showed the Third Estate to prefer the solution more favorable to the peasants. The generous offers of both great lords drew thunders of applause, for which the hundred deputies said by Parisot to have been in the secret doubtless gave the signal; but it was Noailles' formula that was enthusiastically adopted. Serfdom, labor services and all personal obligations were abolished without compensation, while the *banalités*, the rights of *mesurage* and *minage* and above all the "real" fees due on peasant properties were declared subject to redemption. On abolition of privileges in taxation there was no dispute whatsoever.

A Breton deputy, Leguen de Kérangal, warmly congratulated the two speakers. Then the marquis de Foucault successfully proposed a revision of pensions, hoping perhaps to strike at Noailles and people like him. Next the vicomte de Beauharnais obtained a decree promising equality of legal punishments and admission of all citizens to public functions. Lubersac, bishop of Chartres, raised the question of hunting rights, and certain noblemen announced the abandonment of their dovecotes and warrens. Cottin of Nantes moved suppression of manorial justice, after which a nobleman demanded that all justice be free, leading to abolition of property in office. The duc du Châtelet attacked the tithe, which was ordered converted into money payments subject to redemption. Lastly came the turn of provinces, towns and Provincial Estates, all of which renounced their privileges, led by the spokesmen for Brittany and Dauphiny. In all this race for sacrifices the clergy had not especially distinguished itself, a nobleman having been the one to offer up the tithe. Yet the parish clergy offered their "casual" perquisites, thus making the services of religion practically free; and a prohibition was passed on simultaneous holding of more than one benefice and on payment to the Pope of the annates or tribute of a year's income incurred by a bishop at the time of investiture. Thus the reform of the Church of France was initiated. In addition a deputy from Beaujolais, probably Chasset, put through a motion to reform if not suppress the gilds and similar corporations. At the close, on a proposal of Lally-Tallendal, Louis XVI was declared "the regenerator of French liberty," and it was agreed to have a *Te Deum* sung. The session rose at two in the morning. "A contagion of sentimental feeling carried them away," wrote the Genevan Dumont, an eyewitness. The "magic" had worked.

But not as completely as is sometimes imagined. The deputies of towns and provinces followed the example of Brittany and Dauphiny with reservations. In accepting fiscal equality and reform of local administration they showed a strong desire to preserve the "peculiarities" of their own regions, and had warned explicitly that they spoke only in their own names pending referral of the whole matter to their constituents. It was particularism, rather than privilege, that most successfully resisted the contagion.

The resolutions of the night of August 4 were all passed subject to definitive formulation later. Fréteau read over the list on the fifth, and on the next day deliberations began. In principle only matters of form were examined, but in practice the text was disputed and modified in substance. Outside the Assembly, among the privileged classes and at the

Court, consternation and anger were extreme. On August 8 a noble deputy, writing to the marquise de Créquy, expressed his indignation at "a revolution which in fact destroys nobility and fiefs, deprives 500,000 families of their property and prepares France for fetters which we are amazed to see borne by Orientals. The deputies had none of the powers that they took to themselves. They were limited to voting a renunciation of tax privileges. They have annihilated a whole property system." Nor was he the only one to declare that the nobility would not ratify the action of a few of its members. Since it seems that no one of the privileged classes protested on the night of August 4, we must conclude that the recalcitrants either were not present or sensed their own helplessness. But they soon recovered themselves, as was evident by August 6. Several alleged an obligation to consult their constituents, notwithstanding the dissolution of binding mandates. Parish priests spoke up against redemption of the tithe, nobles against redemption of manorial dues and abolition of manorial justice. On the other hand it was difficult if not impossible, because of the juridical complexities of feudal law, to draw the distinction between personal obligations abolished without indemnity and real obligations subject to redemption. Opponents of the measures made sport of the embarrassment of the feudal lawyers. But the majority would concede nothing. In fact the uncertainty that hovered over any classification of feudal rights turned against them; the *banalités* and *mesurage* disappeared form the list of dues to be redeemed. If the nobility still had any illusions they were undeceived by the opening words of the definitive decree, dated August 5–11, 1789: "The National Assembly destroys the feudal regime *entirely*." The phrase was far from being exact, for the need of gradual redemption assured that regime a long life, and the honorific privileges and the law of primogeniture had not even been touched. Yet the issue had at no time been in doubt.

Nevertheless the two most prominent leaders of the Third, Mirabeau and Sieyès, had refrained from attending the session of the fourth, though surely informed of what was to happen. It is certain that they disapproved. Mirabeau, without attacking the decree, helped to postpone discussion of the honorific rights on August 6 and of primogeniture on August 12. Sieyès remained silent, but at the end of the month he submitted to the committee on feudalism, created on the twelfth to work out the law regulating redemption, a memorandum in which he vehemently criticized the action of the Assembly. If these two men failed to attack frankly, and in time, it is clearly because they thought the current to be too strong.

It was on the tithe that the debates really grew lively, taking a turn singularly menacing for the clergy, and ending with a decisive addition to the resolutions of the fourth. On August 6 the curates who objected to redemption of the tithe drew a thundering reply from Buzot: "First, I maintain that church property belongs to the nation. . . . The best course for the clergy is to save appearances by seeming to do of itself, as a sacrifice, what imperious circumstances actually force it to do." On the eighth, during discussion of a loan proposed by Necker, the marquis de Lacoste returned to the fray, and in proposing abolition pure and simple of the tithe suggested turning over church property to government creditors as collateral. Alexander de Lameth supported him, while the abbé de Montesquiou energetically defended his order. Thus was raised for the first time the question of nationalization of the church properties. Most of the arguments had been formulated, but it was too soon to come to a decision and the debate remained inconclusive. On the tithe, however, the story was different; when the article concerning it came up for consideration on the tenth, it was proposed by way of amendment to suppress it purely and simply, with the understanding that the nation would provide for the cost of worship, and that those tithes conveyed by the clergy to lay persons—the "subinfeudated" tithes—should remain subject to redemption. The argument then began all over; this time Mirabeau made common cause with the assailants, while Sieyès pronounced vigorously for redemption. In the end the majority adopted the amendment. The tithe disappeared without expense to landed proprietors.

The resolutions of the fourth underwent curious amputation in the matter of corporations, and though the circumstances are unknown to us the reason is hardly doubtful. It is that the artisans and shopkeepers in their petitions had shown attachment to their corporate bodies, against the wishes of the upper bourgeoisie, so that the deputies judged it prudent to defer the solution of this thorny problem.

The debates that took place from the fifth to the eleventh of August, however important, were obviously less so than the night of the fourth itself. In a few hours on that occasion the Assembly had realized the juridical unity of the nation, destroying in principle, with the feudal regime, the ascendancy of the aristocracy in rural life and the element of its wealth that distinguished it from the bourgeoisie. Financial, judicial and ecclesiastical reform had also been begun. To the committee on finances created on July 12 were now added, on August 20, a committee on church affairs and a committee on the judiciary.

Doubtless the Assembly formed an exaggerated idea of its work. To the peasants it seemed contradictory to declare feudalism abolished and at the same time require them to go on with their manorial payments, pending redemption, as they were sternly ordered to do by the Assembly in its proclamation of August 10. The aristocracy likewise, disregarding the advantages to be drawn from redemption, refused to accept the new situation, less from self-interest than from pride. Nevertheless the Assembly had swept clear the ground on which a constitution and a declaration of rights could be constructed. The least arguable of all consequences of the night of August 4 is certainly the realization of a national unity embracing all parts of the French territory and all classes of Frenchmen, a unity for which the monarchy had long labored and which it was the glory of the National Assembly to achieve. It is only just to recall the essential role played on that famous night by the liberal nobles, when they associated themselves with the revolutionary enthusiasm of the Third Estate to merge themselves in the nation.

CHAPTER 12 *The Declaration of the Rights of Man and the Citizen*

WITH despotism destroyed and privilege abolished, nothing prevented the prompt drafting of the Declaration, and the Assembly set to work on August 12. Numerous projects had been submitted, and the "bureaus" into which the deputies divided for discussion formulated others. A new committee was chosen, the third, composed of five members, to draw up a text as a basis for the debates. Mirabeau reported for the committee on the seventeenth. Opposition was not yet silenced; some again raised the question of whether a declaration was opportune, and Mirabeau himself proposed postponement until the completion of the constitution. But the majority had decided otherwise, and the proposal of the committee, no doubt compromised by the equivocal stand of its spokesman, was rejected in favor of the one submitted by Bureau Six. Discussed without interruption from the twentieth to the twenty-sixth, it was significantly modified, not in substance (on which there was general agreement) so much as in presentation, the final text being reduced from twenty-four to seventeen articles, and the language becoming more striking, felicitous and concise.[10]

[10] For the full text of the Declaration see the Appendix.

The debates grew excited only on the twenty-second and twenty-third, over the articles which declared it necessary "to the good order of society" for "religion and morality" as well as "public worship" to be respected. The preamble had placed the Declaration under the auspices of the "Supreme Being," but religion was understood to mean the Catholic religion, which enjoyed a monopoly of public worship. Churchmen vehemently insisted that the Assembly confirm the existence of a religion of state, i.e., a privileged if not obligatory religion. Toleration was granted only in oblique language: "No citizen should be disturbed who does not trouble the established worship." Mirabeau protested with vigor in favor of freedom of worship and conscience, and Rabaut-Saint-Etienne pleaded the same case for the Protestants. It was in vain; all that was agreed to was to eliminate the question of public worship from the Declaration, making it a matter for regulation by the Constitution. Attention turned to a motion by the comte de Castellance: "No man may be disturbed for his religious opinions, or troubled in the performance of his worship," but the second clause was dropped and the first gravely qualified. Article x of the Declaration was finally phrased as follows: "No one may be disturbed for his opinions, even in religion, provided that their manifestation does not trouble public order as established by law."

On August 26 du Port obtained the addition of Article xvii, concerning property. The comte de Montmorency proposed that the right of the people to revise the Constitution be included, but this question along with several others was postponed, on the understanding that the Declaration, now fixed in seventeen articles, would be reviewed and completed when the Constitution was finished. But no such revision ever took place, for in August 1791, when the debate was resumed, Thouret objected that the Declaration was now so familiar to the people, so clothed in their eyes with a "religious and sacred character," that it had become a "symbol of political faith" which should be touched with extreme caution. The supplement considered necessary was therefore combined in 1791 with a summary of the Declaration to form a preamble to the Constitution, stating the "fundamental arrangements" which it guaranteed. The Declaration of the Rights of Man and the Citizen, symbol of the Revolution of 1789, remained as provisionally adopted by the National Assembly on August 26 of that year.

Principles

Men are born and remain free and equal in rights. This memorable affirmation, standing at the head of Article I, summarizes the accomplishments of the Revolution from July 14 to August 4, 1789. The rest of the Declaration is so to speak only an exposition and commentary on it.

"The aim of all political association is to preserve the natural and imprescriptible rights of man." Here (in Article II) the idea of the social contract, popularized in France by Rousseau, was implicitly adopted. Sieyès and Mounier had also set up "the greatest good of all" and "the general felicity" as the aims of social organization; but these phrases are not to be found in the text of the Declaration, though the equivalent, the "general happiness," was to figure in the Constitution of 1793.

The rights of man are said in Article II to be "liberty, property, security and resistance to oppression." Seven articles are devoted to liberty. It is defined, in general, by Articles IV and V as the right "to do whatever does not harm another"; its "limits" can be "determined only by the law." On individual liberty there are three articles, of which one is very long, laying the foundation of the new penal code and criminal procedure, two essential reforms of the Constituent Assembly: "No man may be indicted, arrested or detained except in cases determined by law and according to the forms which it has prescribed." Every man is presumed innocent until pronounced guilty; the law may not be retroactive; it may prescribe only strictly necessary penalties. Liberty of opinion, "even in religion," is mentioned in Article x, as has been stated; liberty of the press in Article xi. Property is dealt with only in Article xvii: it is "an inviolable and sacred right," of which one may be deprived only for reasons of public utility as determined by law, and only with a "just compensation in advance." Security is not again mentioned in the Declaration; it simply follows from the maintenance of order as guaranteed by public force, whose use for the "advantage of all" is envisaged in Article xii. Nor is there any explanation of resistance to oppression.

Since the Declaration begins by declaring men equal in rights, it is noteworthy that in the enumeration of imprescriptible rights equality does not appear. Sieyès in his own project had defined it with care, in two articles, holding that there is no liberty if privileges subsist, but that equality is to be understood as applying to "rights," not to "means." Since the Assembly was in entire agreement on these matters, it is strange that the two definitions were not retained, especially the second which would seem indispensable to dispel ambiguity. No article is devoted specifically to equality, but Article vi, defining the law, stipulates that law is the same for all and that all citizens are equal in the eyes of the courts and in admission to public employment, and Article xiii assures equality in taxation.

In laying down the principle that "political association" has the preservation of the rights of man as its object, the Declaration affirms implicitly that government can be no one's property but must belong to all. Sieyès and Mounier agreed on this point, the latter having declared explicitly that government is created "in the interest not of those who govern but of those who are governed." It follows that all authority emanates from the associated people and is subject to their control, for otherwise their rights would be without fundamental guarantees. This is the meaning of the national sovereignty proclaimed in Article III: "The principle of all sovereignty rests essentially in the nation. No body and no individual may exercise authority which does not emanate from the nation expressly." Hence "law is the expression of the general will. All citizens have the right to take part, in person or by their representatives, in its formation" (Article VI). They vote taxes in the same way (Article XIV). Every public agent is accountable for his conduct in office (Article XV). On the organization of government the Declaration prescribes only one principle: the *powers* of government, legislative, executive and judicial, must be separated (Article XVI).

Backward and Forward Looks

It is a commonplace of counterrevolutionary polemics to find fault with the Declaration for being too philosophical and abstract. In reality it bears the strong imprint of the circumstances surrounding its birth; its "historical" character is evident both in what it includes and in what it omits, and in the unequal importance which it obviously places on different principles. If the patriots disregarded objections of whose cogency they were well aware, if they held to the idea of promulgating a Declaration, it is because in their eyes it had an especially great *negative* value, in the sense that it condemned the practices of the Old Regime and prevented their revival. Its formulation of principles is in general terms, as is customary in legislative documents—nor were the American declarations any different in this respect—but for the members of the National Assembly and their contemporaries there was nothing abstract or even properly philosophical in such generalization, for under each article they mentally aligned concrete particularities from which they had suffered. Sovereignty belongs to the nation—i.e., France is no longer the property of the king. No obedience is owed except to the law—i.e., the arbitrary will of the king, and of his ministers and agents, is binding on no one. No man may be arrested or detained except by law—i.e., there shall be no more arrest by administrative orders merely. The accused is innocent until pronounced guilty—i.e., no restoration of torture. Citizens are equal before the law—i.e., there is no justification for the privileges. Resistance to oppression is allowable—i.e., the insurrection of July 14 was legitimate. And so on and on. As the historian Aulard put it, the Declaration is essentially the *death certificate of the Old Regime.*

This is why the preamble asserts that "ignorance, disregard or contempt of the rights of man are the sole causes of public misfortunes and governmental corruption," and that henceforth the citizens, by comparing the actions of government with "the aim of all political institutions," may "found their demands on simple and incontestable principles." It is also for the reasons suggested above that the Assembly did not favor the deductive order adopted by Sieyès, a true theoretical philosopher, or yet enumerate the various principles in the order we should prefer today, or with uniform emphasis. We have seen with what caution religious toleration was provided for, where to us it seems that freedom of conscience and worship deserve first place, or at least the most straightforward affirmation. If the Assembly judged otherwise, it was not only from a wish to spare the patriotic lower clergy, but also because many of the grievance-lists were indifferent to Protestants, hostile to Jews and outspokenly in favor of maintaining the preeminence of Catholicism;

and also because the Assembly itself, being not at all "laic" in the present sense of the word, did not dream of depriving the Catholic Church (as was soon proved) of its monopoly of public worship, birth and marriage records, education and poor relief, but intended instead to bring the Church more closely than ever into the government of the State. Similarly, it would certainly be thought necessary today to insist upon the right of property and to define it and justify it, as Sieyès had done. The Assembly did not trouble to do so because it was a right which the Old Regime did not question. On the contrary, ministers and administrators of the eighteenth century always spoke of property with respect, in an altogether bourgeois manner. Property rights were appealed to by the aristocracy to defend their position as manorial lords. The only concrete complaint concerning property under the Old Regime was that the public authorities were often highhanded in making expropriations on the ground of public utility, negligent in compensating the owners, arbitrary in assessing values and slow in payment; and these are the faults aimed at in Article xvii, which at the same time was probably intended to legitimatize the requirement that the peasants should buy up the manorial dues. On the other hand, individual liberty is the subject of three articles, because administrative arrest and abuses of criminal procedure were a menace to all. The rule of law was insisted upon because under the Old Regime there was no legal requirement which might not be somehow evaded at the King's discretion. Equality of rights was treated at length because special privilege was the foundation of the social hierarchy. The thought in the Declaration looked to the past more than the future.

Nor are the silence in the Declaration less revealing. If there is any principle we should expect to find in it, it is the economic freedom which the bourgeoisie held to above all others. It will be sought in vain. One reason is that the Old

Regime, since the suppression of gilds by Turgot and the removal of controls on the grain trade by Brienne, was no longer hostile to economic freedom. Another reason was division within the Third Estate itself on the matter of gilds and similar bodies.

The Declaration says nothing of the right of association, not because the Assembly meant to prohibit it purely and simply, for the clubs became one of the most solid pillars in revolutionary organization, but rather because it was inopportune to proclaim a right of association at a time when the clergy was to cease to be a "body," and when suppression of property in office was to put an end to the judicial "bodies" also.

The rights of assembly and petition, so much used by the revolutionaries themselves at the very moment, were likewise passed over in silence. Nor was anything said, though Sieyès had foreseen the question, of education and relief of the needy. These were matters of importance for the society of the future, not for the destruction of the Old Regime. They could wait, and were in fact comprised in Section Two of the Constitution as completed in 1791, because at that time the Assembly was oriented mentally toward the future, whereas in August 1789 its members were still hypnotized by the past.

Yet the past could not be separated from the future. Although the Declaration in the minds of its authors had for the moment an essentially negative meaning, it was none the less drawn up in a positive form, in which the preamble especially, while recalling what was to be condemned in the old order, indicated that the principles of the new order were also to be laid down. In this sense, too, in the eyes of the Assembly, the Declaration had a concrete meaning. They knew the kind of organization they wanted for France, and consequently how the principles proclaimed in the Declaration should be interpreted in practice. But whereas interpretation was not open to doubt when matters of the past were concerned, because everyone knew what was aimed at, it was subject to controversy when it turned to the future, since the future was still undetermined and was to be settled only by the Constitution itself. Principles expressed in general terms might be, in the judgment of many, logically contradictory to the arrangements made in the Constitution. Hence the strong current in favor of postponement: if one waited until the concrete task was accomplished, then the terms of the Declaration of Rights might be so adjusted as to be entirely consistent with it.

There is no foundation to the charge often made against the National Assembly, that it incited people to believe in an unlimited and arbitrary liberty and to demand a perfect equality. From Article IV it follows expressly that liberty is limited by law, and the first article stipulates than men are equal *in rights*, an equality carefully defined in other articles as an equality before the law. Nor would we be rash to suppose that the Assembly, in deciding not to mention "general felicity" as the purpose of political association, wished to prevent the transformation of juridical or civil equality into social equality, and to forestall those who might appeal to equality in demanding improvement of the lot of the poor. Even these precautions were not generally considered sufficient. Some deputies, notably churchmen such as Grégoire, suggested that the Declaration of Rights be supplemented with a Declaration of Duties; they were told that rights and duties were correlative, the right to liberty necessarily implying the duty to respect the liberty of others, as was set forth in Article IV. But in any case it is certain that the leaders of the Assembly felt no apprehension at the time. This is not because having read Rousseau they believed man by nature good—they were far more realistic than is often supposed. It is rather that they represented a triumphant class, full of energy and on the way to transforming the world. The bourgeoisie had no doubts of itself, nor did it doubt that the new order it had conceived, in accord with the laws of nature and the divine will, was destined forever to assure the welfare and progress of the human race. Warnings produced simply incredulity.

Yet the warnings were justified. From the standpoint of the bourgeoisie it would have been prudent to adopt the distinction drawn by Sieyès between equality of *rights* and equality of *means*. It would have been wise to include a definition of property. Without these safeguards the Declaration, if examined on a philosophical level and without regard to historical circumstances, can readily be interpreted in a socialistic sense, as was recognized by Aulard. And this is what has in fact happened.

Moreover, though liberty of the individual may imply a corresponding obligation toward other individuals, nothing in the Declaration affirms the obligations of all individuals to the national community. Such obligations may certainly be prescribed by law through restrictions on the rights of man in time of emergency; more than once, in fact, *habeas corpus* has been suspended in England and the state of siege declared in France. The Declaration might therefore well have stated that the right to liberty varies with circumstances, and that circumstances are to be judged by the community itself. This is what several deputies maintained in connection with the repression of counterrevolutionaries. Gouy d'Arsy had already argued that human rights could not be the same in wartime as in peace, and the same doctrine in 1793 and 1794 was to justify the emergency government of the Terror.

Yet nothing of this relativity of individual rights was retained in the Declaration. Silence on the matter was due to the circumstances. On the one hand, it was unnecessary to remind the Third Estate of its duties to itself or of its obligations under conditions of war, at a time when it had declared that it alone constituted the national community, when it was imposing an unqualified solidarity on its members and when it was in process of resisting all enemies both within and outside its ranks. On the other hand, since the rights of man had been invoked to destroy despotism and privilege, it was politically unwise to weaken their force by noting that in some eventualities they would have to be restricted.

But it is incumbent on us, who regard the Declaration as the foundation of constitutional law, so to understand and expound it as to forestall the objection that it contradicts certain practical necessities of social life. We must show its consistency with emergency needs. Our commentary must break the self-imposed silence of the Constituents, reestablish the ultimately relative character of the Declaration, admit the power inherent in the nation to restrict liberty when necessary for the public safety. Such a commentary would be entirely acceptable to the Constituents, who refrained from making it themselves only for practical reasons. The fact is, contrary to what is often maintained, that we cannot explain what the Constituents did and said simply as the result of abstract philosophical prepossessions, but only by taking account of the historical circumstances in which they acted.

It is likewise because they were affected by circumstances that they included the right of resistance to oppression in the Declaration. They intended by including it to legitimatize the insurrection of July 14, or a future insurrection if the Court should renew its appeal to force, and in fact did thus justify the October Days in advance. Had they been merely reasoning in the abstract they would probably have left out the right of resistance to oppression, since it was inconceivable to them, or at least highly inlikely, that any oppression could exist in the constitutional order which they were about to establish.

Of more immediate significance were the contradictions which soon revealed themselves between certain articles of the Declaration and the constitutional ideas developed by the Assembly. "All citizens," according to Article vi, "have the right to take part, *in person* or by their representatives," in the formation of the law. And Article xiv: "Citizens have the right, by themselves or through their representatives," to vote taxes. The phrase "in person" seemed to authorize the direct democracy attempted by the electoral districts of Paris. But the Assembly certainly meant to organize a purely *representative* government. The completed Constitution was not even submitted in 1791 to popular ratification. The legislature became the almost absolute master of the community. Amendment of the Constitution was surrounded with such formalities as to be impossible in less than ten years, and in addition the initiative had to come from the legislators, not from the people. As early as the law of December 12, 1789, there seemed to be a violation of Article vi. That article, referring to *all* citizens, seemed to call for universal suffrage, whereas the Assembly by the law of December 12 withheld the vote from those citizens whom it designated as "passive," those who did not pay taxes equal in value to three days' wages.

This inconsistency might have been avoided had the Declaration included an article prepared by Sieyès in July, which distinguished "active" from "passive" citizens, and which held voting to be a public function to which all were admissible, if only they could meet, as for any public function, the conditions prescribed by law as a guarantee of capacity. This was the doctrine half a century later of Guizot and Royer-Collard; the bourgeoisie reasoned in 1789 as later under Louis-Philippe. But in 1789 the democratic movement was not yet born, and the bourgeoisie expressed its thought in less measured and prudent language than it used later, since it did not foresee that its own political ascendancy would ever be questioned, and since even the Americans, who expressed themselves in the same way, were far from having arrived at universal suffrage.

Avoidance of such inconsistencies would indeed not have checked the course of history. The common people had fought to destroy the Old Regime and had forced the abolition of feudalism. It was chimerical to suppose that they would let themselves be excluded forever from the vote, in the name of a declaration which proclaimed men equal in rights. But thanks to the superb confidence of the bourgeoisie, its Declaration could become a charter of political and even social democracy, since it neither condemned the regulation of economic life nor subjected the right of property to any definition.

PART VI ⊕ THE OCTOBER
DAYS

CHAPTER 13   *The Revolutionary*
Solution in
the Balance

The King's Passive Resistance

THOUGH Louis XVI had capit-
ulated in the face of insurrection, he was not yet resigned to
accepting all the acts of the Assembly without resistance.
The infectious enthusiasm of the night of August 4 left him
cold. On the fifth he wrote Monseigneur Dulau, archbishop
of Arles: "I will never consent to the spoliation of my clergy
or of my nobility. I will not sanction decrees by which they
are despoiled." When the decree of August 5–11 was submitted to him he remained silent. He was equally uncommu-
nicative on the Declaration. A decree of August 10, requiring
officers and soldiers to take an oath "to the Nation, the king
and the law" was even more a thorn in his side.

The Assembly was embarrassed. Until now its members
had not doubted that their decrees needed the king's approval.
But if he had the right to reject the decree of August 5–11 and
the Declaration, and later all the constitutional labors of the
Assembly, the Old Regime would come back to life at least in
part, for to gain the king's support the Assembly would have
to compromise with the aristocracy, and this was precisely
what the patriot party refused even to consider.

For over a month the Assembly would not admit that it faced a blank wall, which might have to be hurdled by a new bound of revolutionary action. On September 4 Mounier proposed an evasion of the issue: "The king would have no right to oppose the establishment of a constitution; he must sign and ratify it for himself and his successors. Having an interest in its provisions he might insist upon certain changes, but if these were contrary to public liberty the Assembly would have two forms of recourse: it could refuse to grant taxes, and it could refer to its constituents, for certainly the Nation has a right to use any means necessary to its liberty. The committee on the constitution has thought that the king's right to ratify the Constitution should not even be discussed." And on September 11 the Assembly took no action when Guillotin asked for clarification of the king's power to refuse consent to the Constitution. But this time Mounier was more explicit: "The Constitution needs no royal approval, for it is anterior to the monarchy." And Mirabeau, by approving the way in which a "religious veil" was thrown over the whole difficulty, implicitly affirmed the sovereignty of the constituent power.

A few days later the Assembly granted the king a suspensive veto in legislation. The Right regarded the decree of August 5–11 as a legislative enactment, not a constitutional matter. To dispel the equivocation Barnave and Le Chapelier on the twelfth, declaring explicitly that the king's approval was not required for the decree, proposed that he be requested simply to "promulgate" it. Mirabeau argued forcefully that the decree was constitutional in nature and so not subject to royal sanction. The debate was turbulent, and not concluded until the fourteenth. But the Assembly drew back, deciding to submit the decree for the king's approval.

Its reserve may have been due to negotiations then in progress behind the scenes on the subject of the veto. The patriot party had agreed to allow the king a suspensive veto on the understanding that in return he ratify all the August acts. Thus the "veil" would not have to be lifted. But on the seventeenth the king gave a procrastinating answer, concluding, after many detailed observations: "I approve the greater number of these articles and will sanction them when they are drafted into acts of legislation." It was in vain that Le Chapelier, Mirabeau, Guillotin, Robespierre and the duc de La Rochefoucauld pointed out that all that had been asked of the king was promulgation.

On September 19 the Assembly passed a motion of du Port requesting the king to order "publication" of the decree. This the king granted two days later, but his message made it clear that publication was not tantamount in his eyes to promulgation, still less to ratification, and that it did not render the decree enforceable at law.

Finally on October 1, when a committee on financial planning was appointed, Barnave proposed that it should not begin work until after ratification of the constitutional decrees, and Mirabeau persuaded the Assembly to submit these decrees for the king's "acceptance." The Right took the position that such acceptance, being obligatory on the king, did not commit him to formal approval. But if a legal solution thus seemed nearer, there was no progress in fact; for the king might in fact refuse acceptance as well as ratification. The same conclusion emerged as on the question of the executive veto. Could Louis XVI have been replaced with someone willing to accept an accomplished fact unreservedly, the basic constitutional issue could have been covered up; but since this was impossible there was no way open except to coerce him by a new mass uprising, and such was the origin of the "October days."

Division of the Patriot Party

The king was no doubt encouraged in his resistance by the dissensions becoming evident within the national party, many of whose members had been alarmed by the popular revolution. These included certain liberal nobles such as Lally-Tollendal and Clermont-Tonnerre; parish priests like Barbotin of Prouvy in Hainaut, whose correspondence has been preserved, and who after being vehement against ministers, nobles and bishops passed abruptly to the opposition when he saw, as a receiver of tithes, the better part of his income vanishing; and likewise various bourgeois dispossessed of manorial rights, apprehensive of street disorders and wondering whether the Revolution, undertaken to prevent bankruptcy, would not consummate it instead.

Hence there gradually appeared a group determined to stop the advance of the Revolution or even to push it back, especially since to restore agreement it would be necessary to conciliate the king and the aristocracy, which in turn would presuppose a partial abandonment of gains already acquired. Concessions were not impossible. The decree of August 5–11 had already reduced the expectations raised among the peasants by the night of August 4. To execute the decree it would be necessary to regulate the redemption of manorial rights by legislation, which offered possible ground for an understanding. As for the Declaration of Rights, it was phrased in sufficiently general terms to allow the organization of powers in a way acceptable to the king and nobility. To satisfy the latter the creation of two chambers, as in England, was proposed. Membership in the upper chamber might be at the designation of the king and thereafter hereditary, in which case it would become a bastion of aristocracy; or it might be elective, with the elective power in the hands of a body small enough to be controlled by the moderate party. To the king might be offered an absolute veto, or right to annul the acts of the legislature. With these questions settled, it would remain only to enact an electoral law. The Assembly could then dissolve, leaving it to the future chambers to proceed to reforms, whose detailed character would be kept within the wishes of the king and the upper chamber by the fact that each would have a veto.

Partisans of a bicameral system and an absolute royal veto were dubbed Anglomaniacs or Monarchicals, or simply "Englishmen" for short. To this group belonged Lally-Tollendal and Clermont-Tonnerre, soon joined by Mounier, who now separated from Barnave. Mirabeau also favored an absolute veto, declaring that he would rather live in Turkey than in a country where all decisions could be made by a majority of the legislative assembly. Sieyès was too doctrinaire to favor a veto, since it violated the principle of separation of powers, nor would he listen to any discussion of an aristocratic upper house; but he had opposed abolition of the tithe and manorial dues, and was soon to condemn the nationalization of the church lands; he had ceased to be a source of inspiration to the Third Estate.

A majority of the patriot party—whose leadership now passed to Barnave, du Port and Alexander and Charles de Lameth—rejected an upper chamber, even an elective one, in which the nobility might reconstitute itself as a separate order. La Fayette tried to mediate to prevent schism, and arranged conversations at the house of his friend Jefferson, then representing the United States in Paris. His attempts were fruitless, and in any case on September 1 the moderates let their true position be guessed, for when a disturbance broke out at the Palais-Royal they joined with the aristocrats in asking the king to transfer the Assembly to Soissons or Compiègne. On September 10 the bicameral system obtained only eighty-nine votes, for the Right abstained. It was clear that the Monarchicals had deceived themselves. From the fact that the Assembly had chosen its presiding officers from among their number they had thought that they could manage the patriot party; as for the aristocrats, they had supposed that they would gladly rally behind their banner, whereas in fact the aristocratic party was dreaming of revenge and regarding all who favored compromise as traitors.

On the king's veto, on the other hand, the patriots were by no means intransigent. Barnave on September 2 proposed a suspensive veto, the will of the legislature to prevail if three successive assemblies took the same stand. Necker, told in advance, gave his assent. The purpose of the move is clear. Having refused concessions to the aristocracy, the patriots were trying to form an alliance with the king, granting him a suspensive veto over legislation, with an implicit understanding, which Barnave made clear to Necker, that Louis XVI would give up all opposition to constitutional laws, and would sanction the August decrees immediately and without comment. As for Necker, he saw his own popularity disappearing. The patriots denounced his financial policies, which were based on agreements with the bankers; the Assembly, in voting a loan of 30,000,000 livres on August 8, had authorized an interest rate of only 4½ per cent, which the financial interests considered insufficient, so that the whole operation came to nothing; on August 27 a loan of 80,000,000 was authorized, but further details were left for decision by the minister, so that the responsibility for failure would be his. Probably Necker hoped to get back into the good graces of the patriot party by his agreement with Barnave on the veto. But his difficulty was still the same; he could not control the king's actions. The Assembly adopted the suspensive veto on September 11. But the king, as has been seen, withheld his sanction from the August decrees. The patriots thought themselves swindled. Herein lay another cause of the "October days."

Irritated at such a miscarriage on their plans, and unable to overcome the king's passive resistance, the patriot party came gradually to believe, as Loustalot wrote in his journal, that a second "dose" of revolution was necessary, and that to avoid further difficulties the king should this time be brought to Paris, where fear of the revolutionary populace would have on him the effect of a perpetual intimidation. As early as August 26 the academician Dussaulx, a member of the Paris commune, observed to Augeard as they went by the Tuileries: "When the king is living there, this business may be settled. It was a great error on July 17 not to keep him in Paris. The king's place of residence should be in the capital." When Augeard objected that no one had the right to tell the king where to live, Dussaulx replied, "He can be forced, when the good of the country is at stake; and we will come to that." On September 25 the marquis de Villette, in the *Chronique de Paris*, declared openly that the king must be transferred to the city, and Mme. Roland was of the same opinion in writing from Beaujolais at the beginning of October. But the decision did not depend on the Assembly. Only a mass movement could seal the ruin of the Old Regime.

CHAPTER 14   *The Popular Agitation*

IN PARIS, the new mayor, Bailly, had not succeeded in getting his authority established. The assemblies of the sixty districts of the city, of which one of the most independent was the Cordeliers district where Danton shone, were administering their neighborhood affairs in their own way and claiming to pass judgment on all acts of the mayor and Commune Assembly, which nevertheless they had themselves elected. National sovereignty, to them, meant direct self-government. The organization of the city was only provisional, and the Commune Assembly was to work out a definitive plan, which it was understood that the districts would have the right to discuss and ratify; but since the Assembly was occupied with current problems nothing was done in this direction. Bailly, impatient, on August 30 requested the districts to name provisional municipal officials to assist him; they were to be elected, in two steps, by three hundred delegates from the district assemblies. The assemblies designated the three hundred delegates on September 18, but instructed them to take the place of the Commune Assembly in the administration of city affairs, and meanwhile reserved the election of municipal officers for direct suffrage later on. Thus holding the mayor in check, the district assemblies became bolder than ever. They were in fact sixty popular clubs in which a small minority of Parisians regularly attended the meetings. Through this minority the leaders of the Revolution reached the masses.

The Palais-Royal was still the headquarters of the agitators, among whom one of the most prominent, along with Camille Desmoulins, was the marquis de Saint-Huruge, an unclassed nobleman as much decried as Mirabeau. Even more active were the journalists and pamphleteers. Printing and circulation had become absolutely free. Leaflets and brochures, often very ephemeral, sprouted on every side. Appearing regularly, since July, were Gorsas' *Courrier de Paris et de Versailles,* Loustalot's *Révolutions de Paris* and Brissot's *Patriote français.* In September Marat launched his *Ami du peuple,* whose independence, shown in its genuine concern for the poor and oppressed and in its furious assaults on Necker, Bailly, La Fayette, the aristocracy and the court, won it an immediate success among the small people. Camille Desmoulins still had no paper of his own, but had written two much discussed pamphlets, in July *La France libre* and in September *Le Discours de la lanterne aux Parisiens.*

The questions of the veto and upper chamber led to renewed popular agitation at the end of August, and some began to talk of a demonstration at Versailles to force repudiation of these measures by the Assembly. During the evening or August 30 two hundred men set forth from the Palais-Royal at the summons of Desmoulins and Saint-Huruge. They were stopped by the national guard. Sticking stubbornly to their intention, they appeared before the municipal authorities the next day to demand that the district assemblies be consulted. They were refused a hearing, and nothing happened. But their ideal grew more popular in proportion as patriots became persuaded, both in the Assembly and outside it, that nothing would be obtained from the king without coercion. Juridical disputes were of course of no interest to the people.

If there was popular excitement over the veto, it was because the veto was regarded as a means of blocking the Revolution and as a new symbol of the aristocratic conspiracy.

This "conspiracy," repeatedly exposed and yet perpetually menacing, had been the essential theme of the popular press and popular orators since the fourteenth of July. And in fact the aristocrats were now really contemplating action. A group called the French Regeneration, in which the marquis de Favras and an abbé Douglas were leaders, laid plans for the king to leave Versailles. Louis rejected their plans, but the conviction spread from now on that he really considered flight. Had not even the moderate Monarchicals advised him to transfer the Assembly to Compiègne or Soissons, to which he would presumably follow it himself? This project had been debated in the Council on September 1, and only the king's personal unwillingness had caused its abandonment. But especially disturbing were the signs of another military *coup d'état*. On September 14 the king summoned the Flanders regiment from Douai, a thousand men who arrived on the twenty-third. As in July, he alleged the need of maintaining order. The comte d'Estaing succeeded for a time in persuading the municipal authorities at Versailles and part of the Versailles national guard, of which he was commander, that such was the true intent. The regiment was received with pomp, and the king and queen let the national guard share in the festivities, presenting it with flags. From now on a march on Versailles seemed necessary to check the plot. All Paris began to move. The French Guards talked of going to Versailles to resume their old station at the palace, now occupied by the Bodyguard. On September 22 workmen in the shops at the Military School were on the point of starting. The districts demanded explanations for the calling of troops. The Commune sent deputies to inquire. The danger feared was the same as in the preceding July.

For the "day" now in the making the Paris national guard provided a nucleus of organized force which had previously been lacking. It is true that the popular element had been excised. La Fayette had decided on July 31 to create paid companies with a strength of 6,000 men, in which the French Guards were incorporated. The voluntary guard had been limited to 24,000, and the obligation to purchase a uniform restricted enrollment to the comfortable classes. But at this time their main function was still to assure the victory of the Third Estate over the aristocracy; and the paid guards, the grenadiers, were men of July 14.

It seems likely that the Paris agitators and the patriot group within the National Assembly had some kind of understanding, though neither the circumstances nor the terms are known. Though there is no positive proof, it appears that Mirabeau also, though working for the Orleanist faction, had some part in what was preparing. He thought, like Sieyès, that the crisis would easily resolve itself if the king abdicated and the duc d'Orléans became regent. Probably the duke supplied funds and hired organizers, but if so the secret was well kept. In any case the Orleanist machinations were merely auxiliary, everything considered; we may conclude, with Malouet, that the same events would have occurred had the duke never existed. La Fayette's role has also been called in question, and he has even been regarded as the sole instigator of the rebellion, on the ground that neither he nor Bailly was at the Hôtel de Ville on the morning of October 5, and that he was singularly dilatory in notifying the government of what was coming. This may be only a sign of ineptitude on his part, but if we grant that he acted intentionally we must conclude that, like all the patriots, he by no means disapproved of the popular rising, whatever he may have said later. But so far as we know La Fayette, Machiavellian refinements were not in his line.

While political circumstances thus appear as the essential cause of the October Days, the same thought arises as in connection with the Days of July, that without the economic crisis the upheaval would have been less profound. The women who were the first to march on Versailles, on October 5, complained above all of scarcity and excessive prices.

The Revolution had greatly increased the number of people out of work. Foreigners, nobles and wealthy persons had deserted the capital, bound for the frontiers or the provinces. Some 200,000 passports had been delivered in less than two months. Money was growing scarce; emigrants took with them all the cash they could; merchants with fluid funds transferred them to banks in England and Holland, or left standing to their credit abroad the payments made for goods exported from France. The luxury trades, and business in Paris in general, were badly hurt. Many servants had been dismissed. Charitable institutions were more than ever unable to relieve the unemployed, and the one at Montmartre had been shut down.

Bread remained dear at thirteen and a half sous for four pounds, and could with difficulty be had even at this price. The harvest was good but time was needed to thresh it, and since the granaries were empty there was no available grain. Peasants stayed away from the markets because of the disorders; every town and even every village tried to keep grain supplies for itself, or hold up shipments as they went by. At Paris the authorities met with unheard-of difficulties in procuring the indispensable provisions from day to day, and in milling what they did obtain since the rivers were low and the air exceptionally still. In September interminable lines formed at the doors of the bakers.

The working class, stirred up in addition by the political agitation, began demonstrations to demand employment or increases of wages—the tailors, wig makers and shoemakers on August 18, the apothecaries' assistants on the twenty-third, domestic servants on the twenty-ninth, the butchers on

September 27; and meanwhile the bakers' men threatened to desert their ovens at any moment.

The people, as always, raised the cry against hoarding, and were driven by sheer want, as in the preceding spring, to turn against the aristocracy and the government. The former were blamed for the obstructions and difficulties in the food supply. The authorities were distrusted because the old rumor of a "famine plot" was now more widely credited than ever, now that Le Prévôt de Beaumont, who had been put in the Bastille for spreading the story, was enjoying his liberty. Marat and another pamphleteer named Rutledge carried on a vitriolic campaign against Necker as an accomplice of the food hoarders. To go to Versailles, smash the aristocratic conspiracy and lay hands on the king and his ministers seemed to be a remedy for the popular sufferings. Once more the economic and political crises came together in their effects.

CHAPTER 15   *The October Days:*
              Confirmation
              by Violence

AN INCIDENT created by the
imprudence of the Court gave the signal for insurrection.
On October 1 the officers of the Bodyguard gave a dinner for
those of the Flanders Regiment in the opera house of the
château at Versailles. At the toasts the health of the nation
was purposely omitted. The royal family appeared and made
the circuit of the table, wildly acclaimed, while the musi-
cians played Grétry's popular air, *O Richard, O mon roi,
l'univers t'abandonne.* In the hall and outside it, convivial
spirits wandered about making menacing gestures and
provocative speeches. The national cockade was insulted;
someone cried, "Every man take the black cockade, that is
the best one!" Marie-Antoinette declared herself ravished on
receiving a deputation from the National Guard a few days
later, for black was the color of Austria, hence her own.
Ladies of the Court meanwhile distributed white cockades,
white being the Bourbon color.

Paris learned of the banquet on Saturday, October 3. The
insult was taken to announce a new move against the Assembly and against Paris. Marat advised the concentration of
canon at the Hôtel de Ville and powder at Essonnes. The district assemblies went into permanent session; the Cordeliers

district, on Danton's initiative, ordered prosecution for the crime of *lèse-nation* of anyone wearing any but the tricolor cockade. The Commune was urged to demand the removal of the Flanders Regiment. It forbade the wearing of any emblem except "the cockade of red, white and blue."

On Sunday the fourth a crowd swarmed at the Palais-Royal. Women were unusually numerous and declared their intention of marching to Versailles the next day; they were particularly vituperative against the queen. The National Guard broke up these assemblages, but listlessly and without conviction. That the morrow would be stormy was obvious. Yet La Fayette took no especial precautions.

On Monday groups of women from the Faubourg Saint-Antoine and the public markets gathered at eight in the morning before the Hôtel de Ville. It was not by chance. A popular movement, if concerted, however imperfectly, supposes, if not a single head or directing committee, at least a number of organizers; but their names and activities in the present case have escaped us.

These women demanded bread. Bailly and La Fayette being absent, they lost no time in deciding to go to Versailles. They invaded the Hôtel de Ville, which was practically unguarded, pillaged it for arms and invited a man named Maillard to lead their procession. He was an active member of the "Volunteers of the Bastille," composed of the combatants of July 14 organized in military fashion. Probably he had not foreseen the present movement in the light of a feminine demonstration, for he tried to parley; in vain, however, for he finally yielded. On the way many more women joined the first, willingly or by force. In the rain, to the number of six or seven thousand, if we can believe Maillard, they set forth by way of Sèvres, where the shops were plundered.

Toward noon grenadiers appeared at the Hôtel de Ville, where there remained only a few laggards, who were dispersed.

But when La Fayette at last arrived the guardsmen sent him a deputation to declare that they too wished to go to Versailles to avenge the insult to the cockade. This time the political aspect of the movement became apparent. "The king is fooling us all, you included," cried a guardsman. "He should be deposed; his boy should be king, and you should be regent. Then things will go better." Meanwhile the tocsin was ringing through the city, the district assemblies were meeting and the National Guard was pouring into the Place de Grève shouting, "To Versailles!" On horseback at the door of the Hôtel de Ville La Fayette harangued the multitude without effect; he assures us in his memoirs that he was finally threatened with the lantern. Toward four o'clock the Commune authorized him to proceed with the march. Attached to him were two commissioners who had among other requests to invite the king to take up his residence in Paris. At about five o'clock at least 20,000 men, national guardsmen and others, took the road to Versailles.

At Versailles the Assembly had met in the morning, and the king had just announced, in reply to the request of October 1, that he acceded to the August and September decrees; but his adherence was conditional, for he observed that the Constitution could not be properly judged until it was completed, and that in any case it was essential for the executive power to remain "in full force in the hands of the monarch." The old discussion was launched again, Robespierre and Barère maintaining that the Constitution stood in no need of the king's approval, while Mirabeau once again asked for "acceptance" pure and simple. Mirabeau prevailed; the Assembly was still determined not to rend the veil. At four o'clock, before the deputation of the Paris Commune had left Paris, the women presented themselves at the doors of the Assembly, wet and bedraggled. Maillard was admitted at the head of a delegation; he complained of the food shortage and demanded removal of the Flanders Regiment, but said nothing of the

king. The Assembly avoided compromising itself; it decided
that after acceptance of the decrees its presiding officer,
Mounier, should ask the government to take measures to provision Paris.

Louis XVI had gone hunting, as was his custom. The
minister Saint-Priest, forewarned by private channels, had
sent him a message and summoned the Bodyguard of some
six hundred men, together with the Flanders Regiment, to
the château. The king returned about three in the afternoon
and met immediately with the council. The government still
had no official information, for La Fayette had waited until
two or three o'clock to dispatch his message. No one knew
exactly what the women wanted, but at three o'clock it
seemed easy to block their approach at the Sèvres and Saint-
Cloud bridges, and three battalions of Swiss could arrive
from Courbevoie on short notice. Saint-Priest, while favoring immediate action, added that the king had best retire as
soon as possible to Rambouillet, where two hundred cavalrymen were stationed. The council supported him, though
Necker objected, denying the reality of the danger, and
protesting that civil war would ensue, with no funds available to conduct it. Louis XVI adjourned the council to consult the queen. At about five-thirty the women reached the
gates of the palace, where they were stopped by the Bodyguard. Some were allowed to come in with Mounier and his
colleagues to speak with the king, who received them gra-
ciously and promised grain for Paris, along with all the
bread that could be found in Versailles. They withdrew
delighted, but since they had nothing in writing the main
body of women were annoyed and greeted them with
threats, so that they were obliged to return and implore a
note written in the king's hand. Some of the crowd then
started back to Paris with Maillard. La Fayette's message had
at last arrived, but since it had been written before the
departure of the national guardsmen it naturally said

nothing of that occurrence. The king, rid of the women, thought himself extricated from the affair. The troops were ordered back to their barracks. As the Bodyguard filed out, about eight in the evening, there was some friction between it and the National Guard of Versailles, but the incidents came to nothing, and the Versailles guardsmen likewise withdrew. In short, the intervention of the women had accomplished nothing. The essential question had not even been raised.

Suddenly a little after nine two officers arrived, sent ahead by La Fayette from Auteuil. The council met again. This time no resistance could be considered. Though La Fayette had not said explicitly that the Paris guardsmen had come to take back the king, Saint-Priest none the less insisted on immediate flight, in which Mounier and the queen agreed, so that the king consented. Saint-Priest gave the necessary orders and set off on horseback for Rambouillet with a carriage containing his family. But he was soon overtaken by a courier; Louis XVI had changed his mind and decided to stay. Louis had been very hesitant in consenting to go, repeating with great repugnance, "A fugitive king!" Perhaps he feared to precipitate a civil war in which his most devoted followers might be the first victims. But it must be added that he was ignorant of the intentions of the new arrivals, and could think that the constitutional decrees were the only matter at issue: he might disarm the adversary by being the first to act. In fact, toward ten o'clock, he sent word to Mounier of his acceptance pure and simple.

The Assembly, in its Hall of the Menus Plaisirs, had meanwhile been invaded and was attempting to deliberate in an uproar. La Fayette arrived at eleven in the evening. After attending to the quartering of his forces, and making arrangements with Mounier, he went up to the château, where he was well received by the king. The commissioners from the Commune delivered their message. It was agreed without difficulty that the National Guard should occupy the outdoor stations at the palace, the Bodyguard those inside. Orders having been given to provision Paris, and the constitutional decrees having been accepted, the commissioners had no more to ask except the king's removal to the capital. It was the first time during the whole day that this matter had been mentioned to Louis XVI. He gave no reply. The night was growing late, and a halt was called until morning.

The Assembly adjourned at 3:00 A.M. It alone had gained a substantial advantage from the day's events, for the king had "accepted" the constitutional decrees and implicitly recognized that his "sanction" was not needed. Once again a mass movement had assured the success of a juridical revolution. Probably the majority was content. But the Parisians had not incommoded themselves for so little: the aristocrats might again lay hands on the king; the Assembly itself seemed lukewarm and lethargic; the business must be ended by bringing the king and the deputies to Paris and putting them under surveillance by the people.

Since many of the demonstrators had found no place to spend the night, several hundred milled at six in the morning of October 6 about the palace gates. One was found open. The courtyard was invaded and fighting broke out. A soldier of the Bodyguard was put to death; a young workman was killed by a shot; a second guard was massacred. The mob reached the staircase leading to the queen's apartments and got as far as the anteroom, where they were pushed back by the Bodyguard, several being killed or wounded. The queen took refuge with the king.

The National Guardsmen had done nothing to keep the invaders out. Tardily they came in to help stop the fighting, and, taking up posts indoors, managed to clear the château. La Fayette, who had slept at the Hôtel de Noailles, appeared in turn, reconciled the National Guard and the Bodyguard and showed himself on a balcony with the royal family. The crowd, at first undecided, finally broke into applause, but cried, "To Paris!" without budging an inch. There could be no more illusions: after a few minutes the king yielded. At the same time he asked the advice of the Assembly, which replied simply that it was inseparable from the king's person, which in turn amounted to a vote for transfer to Paris.

At one in the afternoon, to the sound of cannon, the National Guard led off the procession, carrying a loaf of bread on a bayonet and followed by wagons full of wheat and flour, decorated with foliage and escorted by burly market men and by women, some seated on the horses and cannons, and carrying branches adorned with ribbons. "It looked like a walking forest, with the iron of pikes and musket barrels gleaming in it," wrote a witness. Next in line came the grenadiers with the disarmed Bodyguard in their custody, then the Flanders Regiment and the Swiss, then a carriage in which rode the king and his family, with La Fayette prancing beside it. They were followed by carriages bearing a hundred deputies chosen to represent the Assembly. In the rear came more National Guardsmen, and the crowd.

All plodded through the mud. It was raining, and the dark came early. The people, insensitive to the gloom of the day, appeased and confident for the moment, thought only of their victory and burst into songs and jests. They were bringing back "the baker, the baker's wife and the baker's boy."

Bailly welcomed the king at the city gate and conducted him to the Hôtel de Ville, where he was harangued by various speakers. Not till ten at night did the royal family enter the Tuileries, deserted by it for over a century. The Assembly took its time about following; it decided on October 12 to move on the nineteenth, and after sitting in Paris for two weeks in the great hall of the Archdiocese, installed itself on

November 9 in a riding school near the Tuileries, which had been hastily remodeled for the purpose.

At the moment no attention was paid to the flood of *émigrés* driven from France by the October Days. Nor was there any alarm at seeing the patriot party undergo its first amputation, by which the moderates, vanquished along with the aristocrats, were thrown definitely into the opposition, with Mounier, their leader, throwing up the game and retiring to his home in Dauphiny, from which he soon moved on into foreign parts. Although all evidence showed the king to be henceforth the prisoner and hostage of the Revolution, there was again a kind of understanding that, withdrawn from the influence of the aristocratic conspiracy, he was now in agreement with the Assembly. During the first days the population showed him signs of attachment. No one dreamed that the Revolution was barely beginning. And, after all, the popular feeling was not entirely mistaken, for the days of October, by securing ratification of the decrees of August, had consecrated the demise of the Old Regime beyond hope of revival, and at least the Revolution of 1789 was over.

CONCLUSION

Conclusion

THE Revolution of 1789 consisted first of all in the fall of absolute monarchy and advent of a liberty henceforth guaranteed by constitutional government; nor on this score can it be doubted that it was a national revolution, since the privileged orders as well as the Third Estate demanded a constitution and a regime in which individual rights would be respected.

But it was also the advent of equality before the law, without which liberty would be but another privilege of the powerful. For the French of 1789 liberty and equality were inseparable, almost two words for the same thing; but had they been obliged to choose, it is equality that they would have chosen; and when the peasants, who formed the overwhelming majority, cheered the conquest of liberty they were in fact thinking of the disappearance of the authority of the manorial lord, and his reduction to the status of a mere citizen. They were thinking, that is, of equality.

Thus made free and equal in rights, the French founded the nation anew, one and indivisible, by voluntary consent, in the movements called federations and especially in the Federation of July 14, 1790. This third characteristic of the Revolution of 1789 was one of its most original features, and the assertion that a people has the right to dispose of itself, and cannot be annexed to another without its own adherence freely expressed, has exerted an influence by no means yet exhausted in the world.

Moreover, the men of 1789 never entertained the idea that the rights of man and citizen were reserved for the French only. Christianity drew no distinction among men; it called on them all to meet as brothers in the divine city. In the same way the revolutionaries thought of liberty and equality as the common birthright of mankind. Imagining that all peoples would emulate their example, they even dreamed for an instant that the nations, in becoming free, would be reconciled forever in universal peace.

In the view of the lawyers, who represented and guided the bourgeoisie, the Revolution was to be a peaceful readjustment, imposed by opinion and translated rather simply into new juridical formulations. And in fact the essential work of the Revolution of 1789 may be found registered in the resolutions of August 4 and in the Declaration of the Rights of Man and the Citizen. But it would be childish to emphasize only these legislative enactments, throwing into the background the events which gave them birth; childish likewise, and indeed more so, to select from among these events certain ones to compose a legend. The Estates-General skillfully and boldly defended the cause of the Third Estate which was the cause of the nation, but as even Buchez admitted, a peace-loving and Catholic democrat of 1848, "The Assembly would have achieved nothing without the insurrections." The Old Regime did not bend before the juridical revolution. Having taken to force, it was destroyed by force, which the people, descending into the street, put at the service of what they regarded as right, though even their own representatives had not dared to ask such assistance from them.

Whether the resort to violence was *in principle* necessary or unnecessary the historian cannot know. He observes simply that in the spring of 1789 the French people still had no thought of it, and that two years earlier they did not even suspect the regime to be nearing its end. It was the aristocracy that precipitated the Revolution by forcing the king to call the Estates-General. Once the Third Estate obtained the right to express itself, the possibility of concessions which would have satisfied it for a time depended on the nobles and on the king. The issue was not so much political in character as social; for the transformation of the monarchy into a constitutional government was a reform on which nobles and bourgeois agreed, and by which Louis XVI would have lost little authority; but the great majority of the nobles, while prepared to make concessions in the direction of fiscal equality, were determined, more from pride than from material interest, to preserve their other privileges and remain a nation within the nation. One wonders whether the year 1789 might not have become the first phase of an evolutionary movement, during which the nobles would have gradually come to accept the status of mere citizens. It is possible, and, if one likes, even probable; but, since we cannot run history over like an experiment in a laboratory, opinions on this question will always be divided. In any case, what actually happened is that the necessary decisions were not made in time, that the Court turned to force to protect the aristocracy and that the problem was therefore presented in all its fullness. The Third Estate, driven to the wall, had to choose between resistance and surrender, so that in fact insurrection became inevitable, considering that fundamentally the Third was resolved to stand its ground.

The insurrectionists knew the risks they took and a few dozens of them felt the rigors of the provosts' courts. In the last analysis nothing except their own audacity, courage and readiness for sacrifice can explain their determination to put their lives in jeopardy and prefer death to eternal submission. Other men with the same reasons to fight have resigned themselves. Revolutionary action takes place in the realm of the spirit.

Still it need hardly be said that many motives combined to bring the French people to their supreme dilemma. We have attempted to single them out. Class interests and personal interests, humbled pride, mass suffering, philosophical propaganda all made their contribution, in proportions different for each individual, but with the net effect of producing in the Third Estate a collective mentality that was strangely complex, but which in summary expressed itself as a belief in an aristocratic conspiracy, a belief which in turn aroused passionate feelings, the fear, the frenzy for fighting, the thirst for revenge that characterized the days of July.

Dismayed by popular excesses, the bourgeoisie tried to blame them on provocative agents, foreigners, "brigands" and criminals such as inevitably mingled with the insurgents. It is true that men who are the dregs of society are not the last to take part in mobs. But the allegations of the Assembly and the bourgeois authorities have a note of apology. The ordinary people neither condemned nor repudiated the murders of July, nor did Barnave or Mme. Roland. The elements in the revolutionary complex cannot be taken apart. In this sense Clemenceau was right: the Revolution is a *bloc*, a single thing. The moralist must praise heroism and condemn cruelty; but the moralist does not explain events.

The irruptions of popular violence exerted on the Revolution an influence that can be indicated here only briefly, but which cannot be passed over in silence.

Without popular pressure the Constituent Assembly would no doubt have pruned down the manorial system, but it is doubtful whether it would have dealt it so rude a blow. Even the monetary redemption of dues, provided for by the Assembly, was not accepted by the peasants, who in the end, in 1793, obtained their abolition pure and simple. If the French peasantry were able to become a democracy of small, independent proprietors, where redemption would have disastrously weakened or even ruined them, it is to themselves that they owed it; they liberated themselves, and the successive Assemblies only sanctioned what they accomplished.

But struck at in its property, after being struck at in its pride by suppression of orders and privileges, the nobility vowed an inexpiable hatred to the Revolution. The aristocratic conspiracy was not long in becoming a reality with all the characteristics that the people attributed to it, including preparations for civil war and appeals for foreign assistance, and it provoked reactions in an ascending order of violence, the September massacres of 1792 and finally the Terror.

The king on the other hand found himself irremediably compromised after turning to force to maintain his own authority and to uphold the privileged classes. Not wishing to dethrone him, the Assembly found itself condemned to a systematic weakening of the executive power, to an absorption of all powers in itself and a virtual exercise of dictatorship, yet without the effectiveness of dictatorship because the executive remained in being and working against it. The Revolution was thus cast adrift until the hour of its extreme peril.

And finally, though the people by intervening saved the Assembly, it is an error to suppose that they shared in a complete communion of ideas with the bourgeoisie. The small people had aims of their own: abolition of manorial dues was one of them; another was the restoration of the old system of economic regulation which blocked the expansion of capitalism, and which the royal government, large proprietors and upper bourgeoisie by common accord and step by step had dismantled in the course of the eighteenth century. Popular insurrection, as at times in the past, forced the suppression of free trade in grains and a resumption by the peasants of their collective village rights, such as reestablishment of rights of vacant pasture and repossession of commons which had been alienated from them. On a more general level, the proclamation of equality of rights only accentuated the inequalities in means, and since these latter resulted mainly from inequalities of wealth, a conflict of mixed political and social significance between proprietors and proletarians could hardly fail to take form. It was to lead the Revolution on to democracy, and was to be decisive, ten years later, in bringing the bourgeoisie to appeal to military dictatorship as a means of restoring the ascendancy of the "notables."

Yet it is no less clear that on August 26, 1789, the bourgeoisie laid the definitive foundations of the new society. Though the Revolution of 1789 was only the first act in the French Revolution, those that followed it in protracted series down to 1830 were in essence a long conflict over this basic charter. The Declaration of the Rights of Man and the Citizen stands as the incarnation of the Revolution as a whole.

Much labor has been spent in contesting the originality of the Declaration, in deducing its substance, for example, from the bills of rights adopted by the American colonists in the struggle that won their independence. The men of the Constituent Assembly were undoubtedly familiar with these documents, especially the one issued by Virginia on May 10, 1776. The inspiration and content of the American and French declarations were the same. It was in fact with Jefferson, as early as January 1789, that La Fayette discussed his project; the text that he presented to the Assembly on July 11, with the accompanying letter, has been found in the papers of the ambassador of the United States, annotated by his own hand. The influence of America is beyond question. But this is not to say that without America the French declaration would not have seen the light. The whole philosophic movement in France in the eighteenth century pointed to such an act; Montesquieu, Voltaire and Rousseau had collaborated in its making. In reality, America and France, like

England before them, were alike tributaries to a great stream of ideas, which, while expressing the ascendancy of the bourgeoisie, constituted a common ideal that summarized the evolution of western civilization.

Through the course of centuries our Western world, formed by Christianity yet inheriting ancient thought, has directed its effort through a thousand vicissitudes toward the liberation of the human person. The Church upheld the freedom of the individual so that he might work in peace for his salvation and entrance into heaven. From the sixteenth to the eighteenth centuries philosophers proposed that man also throw off the fetters that held down his rise on earth; they urged him to become the master of nature and make his kind the true ruler of creation. Different though such doctrine seemed from that of the Church, the two were at one in recognizing the eminent dignity of the human person and commanding respect for it, in attributing to man certain natural and imprescriptible rights and in assigning to the authority of the state no other purpose than to protect these rights and to help the individual make himself worthy of them.

The West, inspired by the same masters, continued also to acknowledge the unity of mankind. The Church promised salvation to all without distinction of race, language or nation. To this universalism the new thinkers remained faithful. They secularized the idea of the Christian community, but they kept it alive.

Both these principles are preserved in the Declaration, for which the free and autonomous individual is the supreme end of social organization and of the state, and which has no knowledge of chosen or pariah races. It appeals throughout the earth to men of good will who cry with Victor Hugo:

"Je hais l'oppression d'une haine profonde."

Many objections have been made to the Declaration. Some have already been mentioned because they apply to the circumstances in which it was debated in the Assembly. Others of more general bearing merit a moment's further attention.

The Declaration, it has been said, is a mere abstraction from real life. Some men may be worthy of the rights it proclaims; some are less so; some, indeed, are hardly human. For cannibals, for example, the rights of man can have no real application; and if it be argued that even cannibals are human beings, still they are scarcely human in our sense. Nor, it is alleged, does the Declaration allow for circumstances. If war or economic crisis endanger a nation's existence, are the rights of its citizens to have the same free scope as in times of prosperity? And if individual rights are not inherently limited, will not the government be granted the power to limit them?

There is no force in this criticism except when the Declaration is confused with a legal code, whereas its nature is that of moral principle, not of positive legislation. We are bound by moral principle, for example—as well as by the Declaration—not to do to another what we should not wish him to do to us. Moral principle does not specify what our conduct should be in each particular case; it leaves this task to the moralist or the casuist. Similarly the Declaration proclaims the rights of man, but leaves to the law, which may vary with circumstances, the task of determining the extent, which may also vary with circumstances, to which these rights may be exercised, always providing that the law is the true expression of the general will, i.e., of the majority of the community. That the members of the National Assembly considered this to be the character of the Declaration is clear from the debates in which, a month before its adoption, they discussed the operations of counter-revolutionaries and considered setting up a special court: governing in

wartime is not like governing in peacetime, observed Gouy
d'Arsy, anticipating Robespierre. Again, when the question
of slavery arose, the relativism in the Declaration became
apparent; it was judged impossible to transfer the blacks
abruptly, without apprenticeship in freedom, from slavery
to the full status of citizenship. And the Assembly reached
by implication the same conclusion for France, when it
made the right to vote depend on degree of economic well-
being, and the right to be elected depend on the owning of
real estate, because, rightly or wrongly, it regarded such economic well-being, and especially the ownership of land, as
the only means of assuring the enlightenment and self-
restraint thought necessary to the exercise of the rights of
man and of citizenship. These rights then are relative to circumstances. The Declaration is an ideal to be realized. It is a
direction of intention.

Another criticism, vehemently raised in our day, is that it
favored one class at the expense of others, namely the bourgeoisie that drew it up, and that it thus provoked a disorder
that threatens the community with disruption. The Declaration did indeed list property among the rights of man, and
its authors meant property as it then existed and still does;
moreover, economic liberty, though not mentioned, is very
much in its spirit. This amounts to saying that the man who
holds the land and the other instrumentalities of labor, i.e.,
capital, is in fact master of those who possess nothing but
their muscles and their intelligence, because they depend on
him for the opportunity to earn their living. The evil is
made worse, it is added, by the inheritance of property,
which endows certain children, irrespective of merit or
capacity, with the *means* over and above the *rights* which are
all that others receive. The Declaration, in short, is blamed
for having allowed capitalism to develop without control
and for having thus caused the proletariat to rise against
it—to have had as a consequence a new class struggle of an

always accelerating violence, all for want of some power of arbitration that can be granted only to the state. Contrariwise, those who deny such a power to the state have not failed to invoke the Declaration, elaborating upon it with ideas drawn from its own authors, who undoubtedly held to *laissez-faire* and unlimited competition as universal panaceas, and conceived of property as an absolute right to use or to abuse.

Here again, for a reply, we must appeal to the Constituents themselves. They had before their eyes a society in which modern capitalism was barely beginning, and in which the increase of productive capacity seemed the essential corrective to poverty and want. Even to those who gave thought to the poor it seemed not impossible that every man might own a few acres or a shop that would make him self-sufficient; and this ideal, which was that of the *sans-culottes*, remained alive well into the nineteenth century. Experience has not justified these hopes. Rousseau had already observed, long before 1789, that democracy is not compatible with an excessive inequality of wealth. It is for the community to examine whether the changes since 1789 in the economic and social structure of society do not justify intervention by the law, so that the excess of *means* in the hands of some may not reduce the *rights* of others to an empty show. By what procedure? That too is for the community to decide, in the spirit of the Declaration, which in proclaiming liberty did not mean an aristocratic liberty reserved for a few, such as Montalambert demanded in 1850, but which rather, confiding to the law the task of delimiting the rights of citizens, left it to take the measures that may be suitable to prevent social disruption.

Finally, according to other critics, the Declaration regards law as simply the will of the citizens; but what would become of the nation if the majority oppressed the minority, or if it refused to make the necessary sacrifices which in time of war may reach to life itself? The community, this school concludes, cannot be identified with the citizens who make it up at a given moment; extending beyond them in time, it is hierarchically above them, for without it they would not exist; it is really embodied in the state, which in consequence cannot depend on the will of ephemeral citizens, and for that reason has the right to coerce them. With this idea, it need hardly be said, we return to the personal absolutism of the Old Regime, for the state, whatever may be said, has itself no effective existence except in individual persons, who by and large would confer their mandates upon themselves. Still less need it be remarked that this system is in radical contradiction with the Declaration in reducing the individual to be a mere instrument in the hands of the state, depriving him of all liberty and all self-determination.

But these answers do not remove the difficulty, as too often we delude ourselves into believing. It is perfectly true that the Declaration carries with it a risk, as do absolutism and dictatorship, though the risk is of another kind. The citizens must be made to face their responsibilities. Invested with the rights of governing themselves, if they abuse their powers with respect to one another, above all if they refuse from personal selfishness to assure the welfare of the community, the community will perish, and with it their liberty, if not indeed their existence.

We come here to the deeper meaning of the Declaration. It is a direction of intention; it therefore requires of the citizens an integrity of purpose, which is to say a critical spirit, patriotism in the proper sense of the word, respect for the rights of others, reasoned devotion to the national community, "virtue" in the language of Montesquieu, Rousseau and Robespierre. "The soul of the Republic," wrote Robespierre in 1792, "is virtue, love of country, the generous devotion that fuses all interests into the general interest." The Declaration in proclaiming the rights of man appeals at the same time to discipline freely consented to, to sacrifice if need be, to cultivation of character *and to the mind*. Liberty is by no means an invitation to indifference or to irresponsible power; nor is it the promise of unlimited well-being without a counterpart of toil and effort. It supposes application, perpetual effort, strict government of self, sacrifice in contingencies, civic and private virtues. It is therefore more difficult to live as a free man than to live as a slave, and that is why men so often renounce their freedom; for freedom is in its way an invitation to a life of courage, and sometimes of heroism, as the freedom of the Christian is an invitation to a life of sainthood.

It is thus through a gross misunderstanding that the Declaration has been portrayed as an invitation to a dull and mediocre life of material well-being; and that in order to strike it from the face of the earth, some people have tried to appeal to our youth and to their penchant for danger and action.

Youth of 1939! The Declaration is also a tradition, a glorious tradition. Listen, as you read it, to the voice of your forefathers, to those who shouted "Long live the Nation!" as they fought at Valmy, at Jemappes, and at Fleurus. They gave you freedom, a noble right that, in all the universe, only mankind can enjoy. They remind you that your fate is in your hands, and that the future of society depends on you alone. Be conscious of the danger. But since danger appeals to you, it should not make you shrink back. Consider the grandeur of your task, but also the dignity that this task bestows upon you. Would you renounce such responsibilities? Your ancestors have confidence in you. It is you who will soon be the Nation. Long live the Nation!

APPENDIX I

Declaration of the Rights of Man and the Citizen

The following is the text of the Declaration of the Rights of Man and the Citizen adopted on August 26, 1789:

The representatives of the French people, constituted as a National Assembly, considering that ignorance, disregard or contempt of the rights of man are the sole causes of public misfortunes and governmental corruption, have resolved to set forth a solemn declaration of the natural, inalienable and sacred rights of man: in order that this declaration, by being constantly present to all members of the social body, may keep them at all times aware of their rights and duties; that the acts of both the legislative and executive powers, by being liable at every moment to comparison with the aim of all political institutions, may be the more fully respected; and that demands of the citizens, by being founded henceforward on simple and incontestable principles, may always redound to the maintenance of the constitution and the general welfare.

The Assembly consequently recognizes and declares, in the presence and under the auspices of the Supreme Being, the following rights of man and the citizen:

I. Men are born and remain free and equal in rights. Social distinctions may be based only on common utility.

II. The aim of all political association is to preserve the natural and imprescriptible rights of man. These rights are liberty, property, security and resistance to oppression.

III. The principle of all sovereignty rests essentially in the nation. No body and no individual may exercise authority which does not emanate from the nation expressly.

IV. Liberty consists in the ability to do whatever does not harm another; hence the exercise of the natural rights of each man has no limits except those which assure to other members of society the enjoyment of the same rights. These limits can only be determined by law.

V. Law may rightfully prohibit only those actions which are injurious to society. No hindrance should be put in the way of anything not prohibited by law, nor may any man be forced to do what the law does not require.

VI. Law is the expression of the general will. All citizens have the right to take part, in person or by their representatives, in its formation. It must be the same for all whether it protects or penalizes. All citizens being equal in its eyes are equally admissible to all public dignities, offices and employments, according to their capacity, and with no other distinction than that of their virtues and talents.

VII. No man may be indicted, arrested or detained except in cases determined by law and according to the forms which it has prescribed. Those who instigate, expedite, execute or cause to be executed arbitrary orders should be punished; but any citizen summoned or seized by virtue of the law should obey instantly, and renders himself guilty by resistance.

VIII. Only strictly necessary punishments may be established by law, and no one may be punished except by virtue of a law established and promulgated before the time of the offense, and legally put into force.

IX. Every man being presumed innocent until judged guilty, if it is deemed indispensable to keep him under arrest, all rigor not necessary to secure his person should be severely repressed by law.

x. No one may be disturbed for his opinions, even in religion, provided that their manifestation does not trouble public order as established by law.

xi. Free communication of thought and opinion is one of the most precious of the rights of man. Every citizen may therefore speak, write and print freely, on his own responsibility for abuse of this liberty in cases determined by law.

xii. Preservation of the rights of man and the citizen requires the existence of public forces. These forces are therefore instituted for the advantage of all, not for the private benefit of those to whom they are entrusted.

xiii. For maintenance of public forces and for expenses of administration common taxation is necessary. It should be apportioned equally among all citizens according to their capacity to pay.

xiv. All citizens have the right, by themselves or through their representatives, to have demonstrated to them the necessity of public taxes, to consent to them freely, to follow the use made of the proceeds and to determine the shares to be paid, the means of assessment and collection and the duration.

xv. Society has the right to hold accountable every public agent of administration.

xvi. Any society in which the guarantee of rights is not assured or the separation of powers not determined has no constitution.

xvii. Property being an inviolable and sacred right, no one may be deprived of it except for an obvious requirement of public necessity, certified by law, and then on condition of a just compensation in advance.

APPENDIX II

Other Books by Georges Lefebvre

The following are available in English:

THE FRENCH REVOLUTION FROM ITS ORIGINS TO 1793. Translated by Elizabeth Moss Evanson. New York and London, 1962.

THE FRENCH REVOLUTION FROM 1793 TO 1799. Translated by John Hall Stewart and James Friguglietti. New York and London, 1964.

THE GREAT FEAR OF 1789: RURAL PANIC IN REVOLUTIONARY FRANCE. Translated by Joan White. New York, 1973. Reprinted as a Princeton Paperback, Princeton, 1982.

NAPOLEON: FROM 18 BRUMAIRE TO TILSIT, 1799–1807. Translated by Henry F. Stockhold. New York and London, 1969.

NAPOLEON: FROM TILSIT TO WATERLOO, 1807–1815. Translated by J. E. Anderson. New York and London, 1969.

THE THERMIDORIANS AND THE DIRECTORY: TWO PHASES OF THE FRENCH REVOLUTION. Translated by Robert Baldick. New York, 1964.

The principal works of Georges Lefebvre not translated are:

ETUDES SUR LA RÉVOLUTION FRANÇAISE. Paris, 1954.

LES PAYSANS DU NORD PENDANT LA RÉVOLUTION FRANÇAISE. Paris and Lille, 1924. Reprinted at Bari, Italy, 1959.

QUESTIONS AGRAIRES AU TEMPS DE LA TERREUR. Strasbourg, 1932.

A full bibliography of books, articles, prefaces and book reviews by Georges Lefebvre has been provided by James Friguglietti in *Bibliographie de Georges Lefebvre*, published by the Société des études robespierristes, Paris, 1972.

Index

226